Avi

by Lois Markham

The Learning Works, Inc.
Santa Barbara, California

The Learning Works

Written by
Lois Markham

Edited by
Kimberley Clark

Page design and editorial production by
Clark Editorial & Design

Cover photo by
Jim Egan Photography

❧

Dedicated to my favorite editor, my daughter Amy

The Learning Works, Inc.
P. O. Box 6187
Santa Barbara, CA 93160

Copyright © 1996—The Learning Works, Inc.
All rights reserved.

Library of Congress Cataloging-in-Publication Data:

Markham, Lois.
     Avi / by Lois Markham.
         p.   cm. -- (The Learning Works Meet the author series)
     Includes bibliographical references (p.).
     Summary: A biography of the prize-winning author of novels for
young people.
     ISBN 0-88160-280-9 (pbk.)
     1. Avi, 1937-   --Biography--Juvenile literature. 2. Authors,
American--20th century--Biography--Juvenile literature.
3. Children's stories--Authorship--Juvenile literature.   [1. Avi,
1937- . 2. Authors, American.]   I. Title. II. Series.
PS3551.V5Z76 1996
813'.54--dc20
[B]
                                                              95-52648
                                                                   CIP
                                                                    AC

Printed in the United States of America.
Current Printing (last digit): 10 9 8 7 6 5 4 3 2 1

Contents

Avi signing a book for a fan

Chapter 1
Beginnings

Avi Wortis baffled the teachers at Elisabeth Irwin High School in New York City. They knew he was intelligent. He read constantly—and he read serious books. His spelling, however, was atrocious, and his writing often didn't make any sense. He left out words, or he put a word in a sentence that just didn't belong there. After almost three years at the small private school, where teachers stressed writing and students got lots of individual attention, Avi's writing had not improved one bit. Clearly, a conference with his parents was in order.

Dr. and Mrs. Wortis came when requested. They had high aspirations for all three of their children. If Avi's writing was holding him back, they wanted to do something about it. At the end of the conference, his teacher and parents agreed—Avi would benefit from having a tutor to help him with his writing.

The tutor was Ella Ratner, a soft-spoken, middle-aged French teacher. She and Avi met in the book-lined study of her house, not far from Avi's home. At their first meeting, she said to Avi, "Let me see some of your writing." That was no problem for Avi. He wrote a lot, both at school and at home. Immediately he pulled out a play he had written, based on one of his favorite books, *The Wind in the Willows*. Ella Ratner read it carefully. Then she looked Avi straight in the eye. "You know," she said, "you're very interesting. You have lots of interesting ideas. If you wrote better, people would know that."

To a sixteen-year-old boy, who wasn't convinced that people noticed him at all, her words were like magic. If writing would make people notice him and admire him, then a writer he would be. Immediately he started keeping a diary, as he knew many writers did. An entry for March 1955 reads, "I can't wait anymore. I'm going to become a playwright."

Becoming a writer wasn't easy for Avi. As he learned much later in life, he had—and still has—a learning disability called dysgraphia. This was the source of his spelling and writing difficulties. However, since that fateful meeting with Ella Ratner more than forty years ago, Avi has never wavered in his commitment to writing.

Of course, he didn't become a playwright. He became a prize-winning author of novels for young people. This is the story of his life, both before and after his decision to become a writer.

It is not surprising that Avi became a writer, given his family heritage. One great-grandfather wrote poetry; another was a novelist. His maternal grandmother wrote plays as well as a memoir of her family.

All four of Avi's grandparents immigrated to the United States from Europe. Today Avi is not quite sure what to call the places they came from. The map of Europe has changed so much in the last few years that some of the geographical names Avi heard when growing up don't refer to the same places any more. He does know that his father's mother came from an area of France near the German border called Alsace. His father's father probably came from what is now called the Ukraine. His mother's parents most likely were born in present-day Latvia and Russia.

The four grandparents settled in New York City, where Avi's parents, Helen Zunser and Joseph Wortis, were born. Helen and Joseph met in high school and later attended the same college in New York City, where they found themselves part of the same group of friends. Helen and Joseph shared the common bond of coming from families that were full of writers, artists, and musicians. They both aspired to be writers, as well.

After graduating from college, Helen and Joseph traveled together to Europe. Joseph Wortis had become fascinated with the ideas of an English physician and philosopher named Havelock Ellis, and he wanted to study with Ellis. Helen had contracted tuberculosis, a wasting disease of the lungs. She was not expected to live very long. Rather than die in a hospital for tubercular patients, she wanted to be with Joseph. Miraculously, she recovered from tuberculosis, though her health was poor for the rest of her life.

Eventually, Joseph Wortis received a degree in medicine at the University of Vienna. His specialty was psychiatry, the study of the mind. He and Helen returned to the United States, where he set up practice as a psychiatrist and Helen took a job as a social worker. In 1935, their first child was born. They named him Henry Havelock Wortis. His middle name was a tribute to Joseph's mentor, Havelock Ellis.

Two years later, Helen became pregnant again. This time she gave birth to twins, a boy and a girl, born on December 23, 1937. They named the girl Emily. The boy won't reveal in print what his parents named him, though any of Avi's fans lucky enough to hear him speak at a school or library might find out. In any case, he was named. A few years later, when his twin sister first attempted to pronounce his name, it came out Avi. The whole family was delighted. It seems that no one particularly liked either one of his given names. Thus he became Avi, and he has been Avi ever since.

When Avi was a year old, his family moved from Manhattan across the East River to Brooklyn, another borough of New York City. Their new home was on

Hicks Street in the neighborhood of Brooklyn Heights. Avi lived in this house until he graduated from college. The house remained in the family until Avi's father died early in 1995.

One of Avi's earliest memories is a tragic one. When he was about two years old, his mother's dog was hit by a car and killed. It was a shocking experience for the young boy for several reasons. For one, it was his first vivid experience with death. One moment the dog was there, an energetic living presence. Then suddenly, it was not. Perhaps even more shocking was the fact that Avi saw his mother crying over the loss of her pet. Suddenly, the person who had always been the comforter of all his griefs needed to be comforted herself.

Other early memories are happier. On one of his first excursions to the beach, Avi eagerly took in all the new sights, sounds, and smells. Suddenly, as he stood at the water's edge on wobbly toddler legs, a wave rolled in and knocked him down. More surprised than upset, he got to his feet and quickly found his mother to tell her the amazing news, "Someone put salt in the water!"

At the age of three or four, Avi started nursery school at the Grace Church School, just down the street from his home. The school exposed him to more new experiences. One day his teacher brought some cream to school. Pouring the cream into a glass jar, she sealed the jar tightly and shook it for a bit. Then she passed the jar around to the children so that everyone could have a turn at shaking it. When all the children had taken their turns, the teacher opened the jar. As if by magic, the cream had turned to butter. Avi never forgot this experiment. For a city boy, the transformation was indeed magic.

Avi got a good report from Grace Church School. Here is what his teacher wrote:

> *[Avi] is pleasant and cooperate [sic], inclined to be rather reticent at times. He hesitates to take the initiative. He has a good number concept. His speech is slightly infantile—but good in structure and thought.*
>
> *[Avi's] intelligent quotient [IQ] is very superior.*

The teacher had recognized Avi's intelligence, but she did not know that he had begun to teach himself to read. Surrounded by books and readers at home, he had mastered the complex art of decoding written language all by himself. One day when he was five years old, he announced the news to his family. As the story goes, Avi raced into the room where everyone was gathered and proclaimed, "I can read! I can read!"

Avi's home was not only full of the printed word, it was also full of the spoken word. Grandparents, aunts, uncles, and cousins constantly visited one another's homes. Whenever more than one member of the family was in the same room, there was bound to be talk. They talked about politics. They talked about history and philosophy. They talked about books and art and music. And, most important to Avi, they told stories. Some were true stories; others were not.

Avi's maternal grandfather was a famed storyteller within the family. One of his favorite tales was the true story of how he almost didn't make it to America. He was two years old at the time. His father had made the voyage to America to find work and a place for the family to live. His mother was to follow with all of the children. On the day of departure, his mother was standing on a dock in Liverpool, England, waiting to board a ship to the United States. She was surrounded by a cluster of children and all of the family's material possessions. For unknown reasons, she had to leave the children for a short time to attend to some business. When she returned, the youngest child, Avi's grandfather, had wandered off just as the ship was ready to board. Faced with the choice of missing the ship or leaving behind a two-year-old, she began to search frantically. Miraculously, she located Avi's grandfather just in time to board the ship and sail to America.

Avi's father's side of the family was also full of storytellers. Avi's paternal grandmother frequently entertained her grandchildren with fairy tales. Although she told them as if they were her own inventions, Avi later discovered that his grandmother was retelling the classic tales of the Brothers Grimm, which she had heard in her childhood.

This grandmother also told true stories of the old country. The region that she came from, Alsace, lay between France and Germany. When she was a child, Alsace was controlled by France. Thus, its citizens spoke French. Then came a war, the Franco-Prussian War of

1870–1871. Germany triumphed and took control of Alsace. One day, when Avi's grandmother arrived at school, all of the French-speaking teachers were gone. They had been replaced by German teachers. Overnight, the students had to switch from speaking French to speaking German. It was a lesson in tyranny that Avi's grandmother never forgot. It made her appreciate the freedoms of her chosen country all the more.

Chapter 2
War

By the time Avi started elementary school in 1942, the United States was at war to protect the freedoms that had attracted his grandparents to this country. World War II began in Europe in 1939. For two years, the United States tried to remain neutral. However, when Japan attacked the United States naval base at Pearl Harbor, Hawaii, in December of 1941, the United States was immediately drawn into the conflict on the side of England, France, and the Soviet Union and against Germany, Italy, and Japan.

When war broke out, Avi's father joined the United States Navy and was assigned to serve as a psychiatrist for the Merchant Marines in New York City. During the war, he wore his uniform to work every day. However, unlike many fathers in military service, he was able to come home to his family every night. In his wartime job, he worked with sailors who made the difficult voyage across the North Atlantic delivering war supplies to England and the Soviet Union. The supply ships often came under attack from the German navy, and many sailors were killed in the line of duty. Many of the survivors developed psychological disorders from stress and from lack of sleep. Avi's father worked with them to help them recover from the trauma of war.

Even though his father was able to remain at home, war still brought many changes to Avi's life. The United States government feared that Germany might bomb major cities on the east coast. New York was one of them. To make it harder for the enemy to see possible targets, the government often declared blackouts. This meant that at night all windows had to be covered with thick, black curtains so that no light showed through. Some citizens took on the responsibility of patrolling the streets after dark to make sure that all windows were blacked out.

Blackouts made the fear of enemy bombs very real to Avi and the other children. Besides that, all children were required to wear metal identification tags around their necks. If the city were bombed, these tags would make it easier to reunite parents and children who became separated during the bombing. On Avi's first-grade report card, when the war was still raging, he got an S (satisfactory) for "Identification Tag," meaning that he wore his I.D. tag faithfully.

Like most Americans, Avi's family followed the war news with great interest. On the wall of one room in the house was a map of the world. Push pins of different colors represented the troops of different nations. As news arrived from battlefronts around the world, the family would move the pins to show the advances and retreats of each country.

Even children as young as Avi were encouraged to help the war effort. Because so much of the country's natural resources went into building new ships, making ammunition, and feeding and clothing soldiers, many things were in short supply. To make the best use of natural resources, many things were recycled. Avi did his part by collecting scrap metal and old newspapers for recycling.

The war also created housing shortages. Every available nonmilitary worker, both male and female, was busy producing war materials. Workers could not be spared to build new houses and apartment buildings. To solve the housing shortage, many families took in boarders. Avi's family was one of them. Their large house had more rooms than they needed, so as part of the war effort, they rented out one of the rooms.

Avi recalls that one of the wartime boarders was a woman named Millicent Selsam, author of dozens of children's science and nature books, including the "First Look at . . ." series and *Keep Looking*. She and her husband were friends of Avi's parents and when they needed a place to stay, the Wortises rented the Selsams a room.

Another boarder was a medical student, who, much to the delight of the Wortis children and their friends, kept a human skeleton in his room as a study aid. Avi wrote about this boarder in one of his books, *"Who Was That Masked Man, Anyway?"*

This novel is set in Brooklyn during World War II, and Avi considers it his most autobiographical work. In the book, the central character, Frankie, listens to the radio constantly, as did Avi and his brother and sister. The title of the novel comes from an often repeated line in the popular radio program *The Lone Ranger.* Using his vivid imagination, Frankie casts himself as the hero of made-up stories based on the exploits of his favorite radio characters and then attempts to turn his imaginary adventures into reality.

In these dramas, Frankie becomes Chet Barker, master spy. Frankie's friend and next-door neighbor, Mario, is Chet's reluctant sidekick, Skipper O'Malley. With Frankie feeding Mario his lines, the two take on such daredevil jobs as spying on the "evil" boarder, getting Frankie his own radio, and consoling the lovely Miss Gomez, their sixth-grade teacher, whose boyfriend has been killed in battle.

According to Avi, Frankie is not what the young Avi was like but rather what he wanted to be like. In reality, while Avi invented lots of stories with himself as the hero, he never tried to bring them to life as Frankie does in the book. The character of Mario is drawn from life. He is based on one of Avi's cousins, Michael Saltz, who lived around the corner. Avi and Michael visited back and forth constantly. Together they played imaginative games, much like the ones Frankie and Mario play in *"Who Was That Masked Man, Anyway?"*

There actually was a boy named Mario, who lived next door to Avi and was Henry's best friend. Avi and the real Mario created homemade telephones out of two tin cans connected by a long piece of string. Using this primitive communication system, they would shout at each other across the alleyway between their houses, just as Frankie and Mario do in *"Who Was That Masked Man, Anyway?"*

In the summer, Avi's family always rented a cottage in the country for two months. At the time, parents feared polio, a crippling disease that struck children more often than adults. People knew little about the causes of polio, but many were convinced that getting children out of the city in the summer decreased their chances of getting the disease.

So Helen Wortis and her three children spent each summer in a rented cottage in the country or at the seashore, usually with other mothers and their children. Except for their vacation weeks, the fathers stayed in the city to work during the week and traveled to the summer cottages on weekends. One father, an uncle of Avi's by marriage, took on the job of organizing activities. Not only did he motivate the youngsters to clean their rooms and work in the garden, he arranged monumental treasure hunts and Olympic games for fun. Adults competed along with the young people. This same uncle introduced the Wortis children to the popular tunes of the day, which they did not hear in their own home because their parents preferred classical music.

Avi's family was vacationing on Shelter Island near the eastern tip of Long Island in August of 1945 when World War II came to an end. Avi and other members of his family joined a spontaneous parade that snaked through the town in a joyous celebration of the end of the fighting.

After the end of the war, when General Dwight David Eisenhower, supreme commander of the Allied Expeditionary Forces in Europe, returned to the United States, Avi and his family went to see the general receive a hero's welcome at a public celebration in Manhattan.

Chapter 3
At School

From kindergarten through the eighth grade, Avi attended P.S. (Public School) 8 in Brooklyn. Every morning he walked twelve or so blocks down Hicks Street to get to the four-story red-brick building in the shadow of the Brooklyn Bridge. Before school and at recess, he and the other students played in the grassless, cement schoolyard. When it rained, they congregated in a large recreation area in the school basement.

Students had an hour for lunch. When Avi was in the lower grades, he walked the twelve blocks home for lunch and then returned to school for the afternoon session. In later years, he carried his lunch to school in a brown bag.

As an older boy, Avi took pride in being a school crossing guard. Every morning and every afternoon, he donned his white sash and took up his post at one of the crosswalks near his school. There he stopped traffic so that other students could safely cross the street.

Just down the street from P.S. 8 was a candy factory. Among other things, the factory produced Peter Paul Mounds bars, made with chocolate and coconut. When the wind was blowing in the right direction, the students of P.S. 8 could inhale the sweet aroma of the factory's various confections. One day, they got an additional treat. A large truck, delivering whole coconuts to the factory, lost its load. Hundreds of coconuts rolled into the street in front of the school. The news spread throughout the school instantly. Students, Avi among them, poured out of the doors to chase the coconuts down the street. Some got souvenirs and some didn't, but all enjoyed the break from studies.

According to Avi, school wasn't terrible. It just wasn't very interesting. As he recalls, he spent many of his school hours daydreaming. Those who are curious to know how one of Avi's classmates at P.S. 8 viewed him, can read *In the Year of the Boar and Jackie Robinson*, by Betty Bao Lord. Betty Bao and her family emigrated from China in 1947. Upon arriving in Brooklyn, Betty entered the fifth grade at P.S. 8. In her class she met a twin brother and sister, Avi and Emily Wortis. Emily became Betty's best friend.

Years later, when Betty Bao Lord turned her immigrant experiences into fiction, she put both Emily and Avi into the book, though not as twins. Avi is thinly disguised as Irvy, a shy boy who is fascinated with spiders. Whenever the teacher asks if anyone has any questions, Irvy is sure to ask something about spiders. How many ears do they have? How often do they eat?

Equal to Irvy's interest in spiders is his terror of girls. In one scene in the book, Irvy reacts in horror when, in a wild celebration of a crucial Brooklyn Dodgers win, a girl pulls him out of a corner and tries to coax him into a spontaneous tap dance routine. Irvy flees into the street.

When he first read Betty Bao Lord's book, Avi recognized himself in Irvy. He admits that Irvy is probably an accurate portrayal of what he was like during his elementary school years—shy, interested in science, and not too comfortable with girls.

In school, Avi got good to average grades on his report cards. In the first grade, the marking system was U (unsatisfactory), I (improved), and S (satisfactory). Along with the S for Identification Tag, Avi received S's in all of his academic subjects. He did, however, get two U's: one for "Covering mouth when coughing" and the other for "Using a handkerchief." His family still jokes about those marks. In all fairness, though, they have to admit that Avi did raise both of the U's to I's the following quarter.

Despite his good grades, Avi always thought of himself as a poor student. This was largely because of his learning disability, dysgraphia, which made his spelling and writing completely unpredictable.

When he was trying to spell a word, dysgraphia could cause him to substitute one letter for another. Thus, *soap* might come out *soup*. Dysgraphia could also cause him to leave entire words out of sentences. Sometimes he used the wrong word for what he meant to say. Other times, he reversed two letters.

Above all, dysgraphia meant that Avi could never be sure when he had written something correctly and when he hadn't. He might spell a word right and then further down on the same page misspell the same word. An aunt once commented that Avi could misspell a four-letter word five different ways. It made the family laugh, but to Avi, his writing problems were no laughing matter.

Avi dreaded Fridays—spelling test day—and he hated getting papers back from teachers. They would say, "Well, you spelled it correctly here. Why did you spell it wrong here?" Not knowing about dysgraphia, they assumed that Avi was in control of his writing, but he wasn't. He was always being told, "You're wrong." "You're sloppy." Avi was constantly being corrected, as if he could do something about his errors. But he couldn't, because he didn't see them.

Teachers repeatedly told Avi that he wasn't living up to his potential, that he could do better if he tried. He knew that he was trying as hard as he could. The constant criticism made him angry, but it also made him view himself as a failure.

Avi's difficulties with schoolwork were all the more painful because every year he was in the same class-room as his twin sister. Emily excelled as a student. She easily got 100's on spelling tests, while Avi struggled to pass them. Today this situation would never happen.

Whenever possible, twins are put in different classrooms so that they aren't being constantly compared. In the 1940s, however, no one—not even Avi's father, who had a degree in psychology—seemed to think that it might be beneficial for Avi to be in a different class than his sister.

Finally, at the end of the seventh grade, Avi rebelled. He announced that he did not want to be in the same class with Emily. In fact, he knew just which eighth-grade class he wanted to be in—Mr. Malakowski's (or Mr. Mal as the students called him). Mr. Malakowski's specialty was science, Avi's favorite subject. Avi got his way, and he loved eighth grade. In fact, when he graduated in 1951, he won the science award, given to the most outstanding science student.

In spite of the science award and the good report cards, Avi still has trouble realizing that he did well in school. He wonders how much he learned at school and how much he learned in his home environment, which was full of books and people talking about ideas. Did he really do well in school, or did he just do better than many of the other students who came from less advantaged backgrounds? Avi still asks himself these questions.

Chapter 4
School's Out!

Avi was always glad when the dismissal bell rang and he could head home. Even though the Wortis family lived in a residential neighborhood, the streets and sidewalks were always bustling with activity. Children, urged to "get out of the house," gathered in front of their homes to play with friends.

Sometimes they played hopscotch or roller-skated, tightening their skates with metal keys. Sometimes they organized games of stick ball, a city version of baseball played with whatever equipment was available, such as broom-handle bats and rubber balls. Other times they played punch ball, a version of baseball in which the ball is punched with the hand rather than batted. Usually, groups of children played these games in the street using parked cars as base markers.

Avi, his brother Henry, and their friends also formed clubs with great regularity. None of the clubs had a purpose, and nothing much was accomplished by any of them. The fun was in forming and naming the clubs. They called one such club the Junior Marines.

This same group of friends also spent vast amounts of time fashioning elaborate forts and other structures out of discarded wood or from holes in the ground. Their games centered around these enormous complicated contraptions that they could crawl into, around, and out of.

During his elementary school years, Avi had two good friends from school—Dickie Macht and Phillip Schwartz. The three were together all the time, playing at one another's houses or in the street. A favorite activity of the trio was reading and trading comic books. When they were at Avi's house, this had to be done sitting on the front steps because Avi's mother refused to allow comic books inside the house. She thought they were too violent.

Avi, Dickie, and Phillip also enjoyed going to the movies every Saturday morning. In the big, darkened theater filled with noisy, squirming children, the three friends passed several hours watching first a series of cartoons, then one or two feature-length westerns, and finally an action or adventure serial which always ended at a moment of great suspense to keep the audience coming back week after week for the continuation.

Avi also got together with other boys at Cub Scout and, later on, Boy Scout meetings. Although he doesn't recall much about his scouting activities, one memory remains strong—a camping trip that turned into a disaster. Avi used the experience as the basis for a short story he called "Scout's Honor."

In the story, three friends try to move up from the Tenderfoot rank to Second Class by taking an overnight camping trip in the country. Since the boys live in Brooklyn, they plan to go camping in New Jersey, which they can reach by taking the subway from Brooklyn to the northernmost tip of Manhattan and walking across the majestic George Washington Bridge. After numerous mishaps—and after consuming half of the food they brought for the trip—the friends finally reach New Jersey. They are surprised and relieved to discover that this small part of New Jersey—liberally sprinkled with litter—looks much like Brooklyn. Their relief is short-lived, however, when rain, coupled with their own inexperience at camping, turns the outing into a nightmare. Although the story "Scout's Honor," is fictional, Avi says it truly captures the flavor of his one Boy Scout camping experience.

When he wasn't with friends, Avi sometimes wandered over to Harry Oncher's carpentry shop, which was always open to Avi and the other neighborhood kids. They could help themselves to wood from the scrap pile and build anything they wanted. Oncher enforced a few simple rules: Stay out of the way, take wood only from the scrap bin, and don't use the power tools.

In spite of his gruff manner, though, the master carpenter enjoyed teaching the boys his trade. While Avi was laboring over a boat or an airplane, for example, Oncher would appear from nowhere and say, "No, you're using the hammer all wrong. Do it this way." Or, "That's not the way you use a screwdriver. Here, let me show you." Avi enjoyed the opportunity to work with his hands at Oncher's shop. He also liked listening to the conversations of the men who worked for Harry. In the shop, he had a sense of participating in an adult world. Later, as a teenager, Avi worked part-time for Harry Oncher and, though he never got to be a master carpenter himself, he has continued to build things, including the bookshelves that line the rooms of his house in Providence.

Although Avi had little interest in sports and always considered himself unathletic, he and Henry enthusiastically followed the fortunes of their home baseball team, the Brooklyn Dodgers. One year, to their great joy, one of their father's patients presented them with a baseball autographed by members of the team.

During baseball season, Avi and Henry listened to Dodger games on the radio and talked endlessly about the team. Their favorite topic was everyone's hero, Jackie Robinson, who, when he joined the Dodgers in 1947, became the first African American to play on a modern major-league baseball team.

In the summer, when Dodger fever peaked, Avi and his family were usually out of town. In 1945, the summer that World War II ended, Avi's mother and father had borrowed two thousand dollars to buy an abandoned farmhouse on Shelter Island near the eastern tip of Long Island. After that, the family spent nearly every summer there.

To get there, Avi and his family spent hours in the car traveling most of the length of Long Island. The trip would take only a few hours today, but the speed limit on highways in those days was thirty-five miles per hour.

One time, when Avi's family was taking Avi's paternal grandparents out to Shelter Island with them, they stopped to get gas shortly after leaving Brooklyn. Grandpa Wortis got out to stretch his legs, and Avi's dad, unaware that a passenger was missing, drove off without him! Fortunately, when they returned to the gas station to get him, Grandpa wasn't angry.

After the seemingly endless car journey, the family boarded their car onto a small ferry for the ten-minute trip to Shelter Island. Approximately six miles long and four miles wide, with a very irregular coastline, the island featured several quiet bays with sandy beaches, perfect for swimming and sailing. Much later, Avi used the landscape of Shelter Island when creating the settings for several of his novels, including *A Place Called Ugly*, *Smugglers' Island*, and *Captain Grey*.

Today, most of the residences on Shelter Island are summer homes. In the 1940s, however, there were many year-round residents. The house Avi's parents bought was in a community called Cartwright Town, which at the time consisted almost entirely of year-round homes. The residents of Cartwright Town made a living through fishing and farming.

Before the Wortis family bought the house, it had stood empty since 1939. It offered few modern conveniences. An outhouse provided the only toilet. There was a wood-burning stove. To make a telephone call, a person had to turn a crank to attract the operator's attention and then tell him or her what telephone number was wanted. Although there was electricity, the family often used kerosene lamps.

For Avi, summers were lazy, relaxing times, a welcome relief from the pressures of the school year. Sometimes he played with local children. With them or with his family, he swam, rode his bike, or went boating and fishing. He and Henry spent a good deal of time listening to Dodger games on the radio. Most of all, summer was a time for thinking, imagining, and reading.

Chapter 5
Across America by Car

One summer the Wortis family didn't spend their entire vacation on Shelter Island. In 1947, when Avi was nine, Helen and Joseph Wortis decided to take the family on a cross-country car trip. They wanted to show their children as much of the United States as they could see in six weeks.

All three of the Wortis children still have vivid memories of the journey. When they get together now, they can reconstruct most of the highlights of the trip. Their mother had the idea of making a family record of the adventure. Before they set out, she bought a journal.

Each night a different member of the family recorded the day's events in the journal. Thus, each person wrote in the journal every fifth night. Avi's brother still has the journal.

They drove from New York across the state of Pennsylvania via the Pennsylvania Turnpike. One night they stayed over in Harrisburg. That night the Susquehanna River flooded. The family woke up in the morning to find their room filled with water! From Pennsylvania, they traveled across Ohio and Indiana to Chicago, where they couldn't find a room for the night. They ended up sleeping in a hotel lobby, with each person stretched out on two chairs pushed together. From Illinois, they continued on through Iowa into South Dakota, visiting Mount Rushmore and traveling through the lush Black Hills. In Wyoming's Yellowstone National Park, they were thrilled to see real bears and gathered with the rest of the tourists to watch Old Faithful spout. From there, they traveled through Utah, Nevada, and California until they reached Los Angeles. There they visited with relatives, including their paternal grandparents, who had moved west after the war. In California, Avi recalls seeing many orange groves and small juice stands with signs announcing, "All the Orange Juice You Can Drink — 10 Cents."

The return trip brought them home via the southern route. In New Mexico, they spent several days on a ranch in the same area where Helen Wortis had once lived fifteen or twenty years earlier. Oklahoma brought their first sight of real cowboys, but the place that everyone had been eagerly anticipating was Arkansas.

Before the trip, while glancing through *Life* magazine, Avi's father had seen a letter to the editor from a George Anscom of Wortis, Arkansas. Why would a town in Arkansas carry the same name as a family of eastern European immigrants? During their trip, they decided to stop in Wortis and investigate.

When they finally reached Wortis, the family was taken aback to discover that the "town" consisted of a post office and a few houses scattered over a large area. George Anscom had created the town of Wortis so that he could become its postmaster and have a job guaranteed for life. Over the door of the post office a plaque devised by Anscom proclaimed, "Wortis, Arkansas— War-Born, Bomb-Proof." Anscom based his two claims on the fact that the town was created during World War II and that its few houses were so scattered that a single bomb couldn't possibly wipe them all out.

In Wortis, Avi and his family also learned that the town's name had nothing to do with their own. George Anscom had emigrated from Greece. Wortis was the closest English equivalent of the name of his hometown in Greece.

After their sweep through the south, the Wortises headed north and traveled up the east coast back to their home in New York.

Chapter 6
At Home

When Avi wasn't on vacation or playing in the neighborhood, he was at home. Avi and his family lived in a four-story brownstone on a street lined with similar houses. The house had been built in 1838, ninety-nine years before Avi's birth. One floor of the brownstone held the office where Avi's father saw patients. The other three were living quarters for Avi and his family.

When they were very young, all three of the Wortis children shared one large bedroom on the third floor. Later, the room was partitioned so that Emily could have her own space. When Avi was eight or nine, he and Henry moved up to the fourth floor, where they had separate rooms. Their rooms were full of board games, books, and other personal treasures. When Avi's room became messy, he didn't have to clean it. His parents employed a full-time, live-in maid who kept the whole house clean and neat. As they grew older, the Wortis children felt embarrassed to admit that a maid had done their work for them. As children, however, they were delighted not to have to clean their rooms.

During their leisure time, Avi, Emily, and Henry often listened to the radio together. On Sunday nights at 7:00, they gathered around the set to chuckle at the subtle humor of Jack Benny, who could generate hilarity just by his intonation of the word *well*, which came out sounding as if it had several syllables. Benny built his humor around his fictitious stinginess, vanity, and mediocre talent as a violinist. His show was followed by the comic Fred Allen, who provoked a long-running, on-the-air feud with Benny when he proclaimed that the strings of Benny's violin (traditionally made of catgut) would have been better off left in the cat.

During the week, the Wortis children tuned in to such adventure tales as "Captain Midnight" and "Jack Armstrong, the All-American Boy." Captain Midnight, code name for pilot Red Albright, roamed the world battling the evil Ivan Shark, whose goal was to rule the world. The serial, which aired five nights a week, was sponsored by Ovaltine, a hot-drink mix. With a seal from an Ovaltine jar and a dime, "Captain Midnight" listeners could send away for a variety of toys or, even better, become members of Secret Squadrons around the country. Members received badges that let them decode secret messages given by Captain Midnight over the air.

Jack Armstrong, along with his uncle and two cousins, also roamed the globe fighting evil-doers. One adventure in this weeknight serial might go on for months at a time with subplot after subplot. The sponsor of "Jack Armstrong," Wheaties cereal, also offered premiums. For a box top and a dime, listeners could acquire special items tied directly to the current story. At one point, for example, a Jack Armstrong fan could get a pedometer "just like the one Jack Armstrong used" to locate a hidden store of rifles in the Philippines.

Avi was constantly sending off for the premiums offered by the sponsors of various radio shows—decoders, ring whistles, walkie-talkies made out of paper, paper cutouts of western villages—he collected them all.

Besides listening to the radio, Avi and his family also enjoyed playing games together. Helen Wortis was often the organizer. She particularly enjoyed a pencil-and-paper game in which one player drew the head of a person, then folded the paper over so no one could see the head. The next person drew the body, and then likewise folded the paper over. The third person drew the legs. Then the composite picture was revealed.

When they played this game, Avi got to display his artistic talent. Because of his interest in and aptitude for art, Avi took classes at the Brooklyn Children's Museum for a while. One morning, when Avi was nine or ten years old, the family came down to breakfast to find that he had been up early sculpting a lump of butter into the shape of a small animal. (Emily says it was a frog; Avi remembers it as a mouse.) Whichever it was, by the time Avi finished handling and shaping the butter, the sculptured animal was gray. Avi's mother was not the least bit upset. In fact, she laughed when she caught sight of the creative addition to the breakfast table.

The Wortis children also passed the time at home playing card games. With their grandparents, they played a card game called casino. When there were no adults around, Henry and Avi played a card game called war. Occasionally, when the two boys tired of card games, they played an informal game called "let's beat up on Emily," or at least that's how Emily now remembers it. She also recalls that she would run to their mother and ask her to make the boys stop. In general, though, the three Wortis children got along with each other very well.

Although Avi enjoyed family games, he favored reading over all other activities. He lived in a house that was full of books. His mother read to the children often, and both parents bought them books. Avi, Emily, and Henry each had a personal library of books. The children also went to the Brooklyn Public Library every Friday to select books for the coming week.

As a young reader, Avi's first love was animal stories. Not only did he check them out of the library, he also spent his own money buying them. Avi especially enjoyed a series of books about Freddy the Pig, and he still admires the animal stories of Thornton W. Burgess. In his long career as an author of children's books, Burgess published numerous books about such animals as Buster Bear, Jerry Muskrat, and Old Man Coyote. His book *Old Mother West Wind* and its sequel, *Mother West Wind's Children*, answers in story form such questions as why Danny Meadow Mouse's tail is so short and why Bobby Coon washes his food. These simple, whimsical tales were among the first that Avi read to himself.

One of Avi's favorite animal stories is *The Wind in the Willows*, by English author Kenneth Grahame. Avi still has the copy of the book he read and reread as a child. *The Wind in the Willows* tells the story of a group of animal friends—timid Mole, sociable Rat, wise old Badger, and boastful Mr. Toad—and their many adventures.

Avi skipped around in the book, reading what he understood and enjoyed and ignoring the more difficult passages. He especially enjoyed the parts about Mr. Toad. Avi calls Mr. Toad one of the great characters in children's literature. "He's an awful man—Toad—but you love him the way he is. He's so funny." Although Toad tickled his funnybone, Avi identified most with the tender-hearted, shy Mole. Avi still has a few of his other favorite childhood books, such as *Gulliver's Travels* and *Otto the Giant Dog*.

When he grew older, Avi usually chose adventure stories, like the Tom Swift series, on his weekly trips to the library. He was also enthralled by Robert Louis Stevenson's tale of treacherous pirates, *Treasure Island*, and Jules Verne's science fiction thrillers. Avi liked Verne's *Twenty Thousand Leagues Under the Sea* so much that he couldn't put it down. In fact, the first time Avi stayed up all night, it was to read *Twenty Thousand Leagues Under the Sea.*

Avi didn't limit his reading to books. Because he enjoyed science, he also pored over magazines like *Popular Mechanics* and *Popular Science*. With ideas from these magazines, he drew his own designs for jet planes and rocket ships. At one time, he even thought that he wanted to be an airplane designer when he grew up. Even more important to Avi than the airplane designs, however, were the fantasies he had about flying the planes. Now he realizes that his fantasizing was more likely to lead to a writing career than to a career as an airplane designer.

One example of Avi's childhood writing, which he still has today, is a play that takes place in the twenty-second century and features Nick Colt, "avator" [aviator], and his sidekick, Skip. Written when Avi was about nine or ten, the play reveals striking evidence of his dysgraphia. In the space of two pages, the word *scene* is spelled *scean, seane, scenn,* and *sean.*

Years later, Avi returned to the subject of airplanes. In *City of Light, City of Dark,* a comic-book novel, he created a character who builds a life-sized airplane, as Avi had fantasized doing himself so many times. The plane builder then taps another character's magic powers to get the plane aloft and hunt down the villain. Obviously, Avi's childhood fantasies were still fueling his writing and they continue to do so today.

Chapter 7
Family Matters

Even though Avi's family did many things together, he often felt isolated from family members—especially his parents. Joseph Wortis did not show affection readily, and he was particularly distant with Avi.

As Avi saw it, his parents considered Henry a genius and lavished attention on him because of his academic achievements. Emily received a lot of parental attention and concern as a child because she had been born with a heart murmur. Emily was one of the first children in the United States to have open-heart surgery.

Avi feels that his parents often ignored him. He especially puzzles over their failure to tell him that he had dysgraphia. If he had known he had a learning disability, perhaps he would have realized that his spelling and writing difficulties were not his fault and he would have felt better about himself. As it was, he was in his forties before a reading teacher looked at one of his manuscripts and told him that his problem had a name. When Avi asked his father why he and his mother hadn't told him about his disability as a child, his father replied that it had been his mother's decision not to tell him. By that time, Avi's mother was dead and could not provide Avi with an explanation.

Even having a twin did not provide Avi with a close relationship within the family. Avi and Emily are fraternal, rather than identical, twins. Identical twins, who develop from a single egg, are always the same sex and often have extremely close relationships. Some identical twins even invent their own language which no one else can understand.

This was not the case with Avi and Emily. They looked different, had different personalities, and led separate lives. Emily was more outgoing than Avi. It was easier for her to approach new people. As a result, she had a wider circle of friends than Avi did.

There were, Avi thinks now, certain unspoken agreements between them. For example, Avi might have been the one to make sure they got onto the subway, while Emily was in charge of remembering the street number of their destination.

Even though Avi and Emily played separately outside of the home, they did sometimes play together at home. Emily remembers one time when, with music blaring, the two stood in opposite corners of the room and pretended they were prize fighters. As soon as someone said, "Gong," Avi and Emily advanced from their separate corners. But instead of boxing, they danced together in the center of the room.

Although Avi has many recollections of family activities, he also remembers feeling that he was an outsider. This didn't particularly bother him. In fact, Avi found solitude "enormously appealing" and recalls wandering the streets alone and happy. "On the whole," he says now, "I had a pretty happy childhood. I was sort of ignored in many respects." To Avi, being ignored was agreeable. It meant being left alone with his own interesting thoughts.

Ignored or not, Avi participated in the active life of a close-knit extended family. There were always grandparents, aunts, uncles, and cousins nearby. One grandfather was an optometrist. The children in the family loved visiting his shop and giving each other eye exams with the special equipment.

Avi, Emily, and Henry often played with their cousins. During one summer vacation, Cousin Alan invited them to be part of a circus he planned to put on. As it turned out, Alan had already assigned all of the roles to himself. Avi, Henry, and Emily protested. Intense negotiations resulted in a fairer distribution of parts, and the circus proceeded with the participation of all.

The extended family always gathered to celebrate major holidays. Thanksgiving was one of them, as were Christmas and Passover. Why did the family celebrate both a Christian holiday and a Jewish holiday?

Although Avi's grandparents were Jewish, his parents were not religious. Helen and Joseph Wortis celebrated Passover as part of their heritage, but not as a religious event. Some members of the extended family took Passover more seriously. Among them were Avi's grandparents and some of his aunts and uncles. At the family dinner where the Passover story was told, Joseph Wortis sometimes slipped a book he wanted to read inside the Haggadah (the book containing the Passover story and ritual). Avi now thinks this was a mistake on his father's part because it created an atmosphere that was not respectful of those family members who took the holiday seriously.

Occasionally Avi's family lit candles at Hanukkah, but that was the extent of their observance. Instead, they celebrated Christmas, but as a cultural holiday, not a religious one. The United States was their chosen home, and since the majority of Americans celebrated Christmas, so did they. On Christmas Eve, the Wortis children hung their stockings by the chimney for Santa to fill, and on Christmas morning, the whole family exchanged presents. Usually the family bought and decorated a Christmas tree. Helen's father, however, refused to enter the house if there was a Christmas tree in it. Whenever he came to visit during the Christmas holidays, the tree was put out in the backyard until he went home.

It wasn't only holidays that brought Avi's extended family together. They visited one another frequently. When they got together, there was always lots of discussion. Avi describes the atmosphere at family gatherings as "an uproarious sense of debate." They discussed, they debated, and they argued—but not in anger. Theirs was an affectionate sharing of ideas, and every family member had his or her own distinct opinions.

Often the debates centered on the social causes the family supported. They believed in equal rights for women. Indeed, Avi's mother considered herself a feminist. They condemned racism. They supported the labor movement in its quest for fair treatment of workers.

The family's support for causes promoting social justice went beyond words. When local workers went on strike, Helen Wortis volunteered at a soup kitchen that provided free meals to the strikers. Avi listened intently to family discussions about the strike and decided he agreed with the workers. So he emptied his piggy bank and donated the entire contents—six dollars—to the workers' strike fund. This strike fund was divided among the workers each week so that they could buy essentials. Avi's family praised his generous decision.

Throughout the 1930s and the early 1940s, the Wortis family staunchly supported President Franklin Delano Roosevelt, considered to be one of the most liberal presidents in U.S. history. One day in 1945, Avi was listening to "Tom Mix" on the radio. Suddenly the broadcast was interrupted, and a voice announced that President Roosevelt had died. Later, the whole family listened to the news reports about Roosevelt's death on the radio while they ate dinner. Even though Avi was only seven, he was aware that this was an important event. He knew that his family considered Roosevelt a good man and that they felt a sense of loss at his death.

The commitment Avi's family made to social justice came from their strong belief in the principles of their adopted country. They truly felt that all people had a right to "life, liberty, and the pursuit of happiness" and that it was their obligation to work toward those principles. More conservative Americans may have called them radical rabble-rousers, but Avi's family considered themselves radicals in the tradition of Thomas Jefferson. As they saw it, they were true patriots, upholding the principles of the founders of the nation.

As a youngster, Avi listened avidly to the discussions about the founding of the United States and its early history. His mother's father, in particular, enjoyed talking about his adopted country. From all of these conversations, Avi developed a love of history, especially the history of the Revolutionary War period. Not surprisingly, several of his novels are set in this period.

Although Avi often felt alone and isolated from his family, today he realizes what an important effect they had on his interests and his values, for much of his writing is dedicated to exposing injustices, especially those suffered by young people.

Chapter 8
High School and College Days

When Avi graduated from the eighth grade in 1951, he had several choices of where to go to high school. He could have gone to the high school nearest to his home in Brooklyn, or he could have attended one of New York City's several specialized public schools, such as the Bronx High School of Science or the School of Performing Arts. Students who wanted to attend those schools had to pass an entrance exam, but there was no cost for attending.

Avi's parents, perhaps remembering his insistence on choosing his eighth-grade teacher and how well that turned out, allowed him to decide which high school he wanted to attend. A few years earlier, his brother, Henry, had chosen Stuyvesant High School in Manhattan, known for its high academic standards and its emphasis on mathematics and science. Stuyvesant was Avi's choice, too. Unfortunately, it was not a good match for him.

At the time, Stuyvesant High School enrolled five thousand boys. Coincidentally, one of them was Walter Dean Myers, who also writes books for young people. When he and Avi first met, years after their Stuyvesant days, they were surprised to discover that they had been classmates for a brief time.

Severe overcrowding meant that Stuyvesant students attended classes in two shifts. As a freshman, Avi was assigned the later shift. He went to school from noon until five o'clock in the evening.

The unusual school hours and the immense, impersonal setting overwhelmed Avi, who already felt insecure about his academic abilities. When the first report cards were issued in November of his freshman year, Avi had failed every single one of his classes, including woodworking shop.

His parents responded quickly to this nonverbal cry for help. They did not waste time on heart-to-heart talks, nor did they demand promises to try harder next semester. Instead, they informed Avi that he would no longer be going to Stuyvesant High School. They enrolled Avi in a small private school where they felt he would have a better chance of succeeding.

Elisabeth Irwin High School was everything that Stuyvesant was not. It was small—about 250 students in grades seven through twelve. It was personal—students received lots of individual attention. It was also coeducational.

Most important, the teachers stressed writing more than any other subject. They expected their students to write on a sophisticated level. Amazingly, like his elementary school and Stuyvesant, this third school that Avi attended also produced another well-known writer for young people. Norma Klein, author of *Tomboy* and *Confessions of an Only Child*, was a classmate of Avi's at Elisabeth Irwin.

Avi loved the atmosphere at Elisabeth Irwin, but even with the school's strong emphasis on written expression, he still had trouble with his writing. By the end of Avi's third year in high school, his teachers had all but given up on him. Nothing they had done had made a difference in Avi's writing, yet he was obviously doing his best. He studied hard and he did all his work, but he still couldn't spell consistently or write an essay that wasn't filled with strange errors. That was when his teacher recommended that Avi have a tutor to help him with his writing.

Again, Avi felt like a failure. His family was full of writers, and he attended a school that specialized in writing. In an environment where writing was important, he couldn't write. His teachers believed he couldn't write. His parents believed he couldn't write. Finally, he believed he couldn't write.

It was at this point that Ella Ratner, the tutor, told Avi: "You're very interesting. You have lots of interesting ideas. If you wrote better, people would know that." Those words changed Avi's life and reinforced his determination to become a writer. Writing didn't become any easier for Avi, but his enthusiasm and determination helped him to overcome the many obstacles he faced.

Avi still has a diary he kept in high school. The entries for the last half of his senior year are full of references to writing and quotations from books he was reading. In March of 1955, he penned this entry, "I can't wait anymore. I'm going to become a playwright." A later entry mentions that he has to start typing a play he has finished and that he has a "good fist full of essays to think of."

In the back of the diary, Avi listed the books that he was reading—three or four a week, including lots of plays. Mixed in with the titles of published books, however, Avi also listed the titles of his own works.

Avi wrote in his diary about reading, writing, and girls. In one entry he asks himself, "Who shall I take out next?" As Avi now remembers it, his teen years were a stressful time for him. Like most adolescents, he worried about his appearance and whether or not people—girls especially—liked him. He was short and young-looking for his age. This was particularly troublesome to him because his twin sister matured earlier than he did. When the two of them graduated from eighth grade, Emily had reached her full adult height, looked sixteen or seventeen, and was already dating. Avi didn't reach his full height until he was twenty-one.

Although he looked immature for his age, Avi convinced a lot of people that he was more mature than he appeared because of the sophisticated books he read and the ideas he got from them. As he now says, "I fooled a lot of people into thinking I was mature, and one of the people I fooled was myself."

Avi had his first date during his sophomore year at Elisabeth Irwin. Mustering all of his courage, he asked Posie, a classmate, to attend a square dance with him. He picked up Posie, her skirt buoyed by crinoline petticoats, escorted her to the square dance, and brought her home— all by subway. Like most high-school romances of the time, this one lasted only a few weeks, when both Posie and Avi moved on to new romantic interests.

During Avi's senior year, he developed a crush on a girl named Alice. She and Avi had the two romantic leads in a school musical, so there was lots of time for the crush to blossom. During the weeks of rehearsals, Avi made constant references in his diary to his attempts to impress Alice with his writing. Sadly, she was immune to his charms, and the hoped-for romance never materialized.

Today Avi says about his high school years, "I had great romantic aspirations and very few achievements." In fact, at some point, the girls in Avi's class took a survey, choosing the best-looking boy, the smartest, and so on. To Avi's dismay, his female classmates singled him out as the best future husband. The girls may have considered it an honor, but Avi wanted to be seen in a more romantic light.

Avi's only involvement in team sports was during high school. For a while he served as captain of the soccer team, a sport he enjoyed, though the team did not do well. That experience inspired Avi's book *S.O.R. Losers*, about a middle-school soccer team composed of students who would rather do anything else than play sports. As a subtle joke, Avi called the captain of this fictional team Ed Sitrow (Wortis spelled backwards).

During his first few years of high school, Avi spent summers with his family on Shelter Island. When he was sixteen, he went to a Quaker summer work camp on a Cherokee reservation in Cherokee, North Carolina. He and the other campers helped out on farms, dug latrines, and laid the groundwork for bringing electricity to the reservation. Other summers, Avi worked as a dishwasher and waiter at various camps.

Avi graduated from Elisabeth Irwin High School in 1955. Since there were only about twenty-five students in his graduating class, the school didn't publish a full-fledged yearbook—only a pamphlet. Under each photo of a graduating senior, the editors placed a quotation from Shakespeare. The one under Avi's picture read, "He will be surrounded by books."

In the fall of 1955, Avi enrolled in Antioch College in Yellow Springs, Ohio. Founded in 1852, this non-traditional school was committed to educational experimentation. Students were given more freedom than most other college students of the time. For free-thinking, liberal students, Antioch was the place to be. Avi chose it for this reason and because a friend was going there. But, once again, he chose the wrong school. Antioch was too unstructured for him.

Avi decided to transfer to the University of Wisconsin in Madison. The school was large, but traditional, and though his grades were never outstanding, Avi did well enough there.

At Wisconsin, Avi chose two subjects as his major: history, one of his long-time interests, and theater, as preparation for his intended future career as a playwright. Although he avoided English classes and the nagging red pencils of English professors, Avi wrote constantly. He still struggled with spelling. He prevailed upon a girlfriend to give him spelling lessons, which were only moderately successful.

Each year the university sponsored a playwriting contest. Students submitted their manuscripts without names on them so that the judges would not be swayed by knowing the authors. The judges evaluated and critiqued each manuscript. Their comments were then returned to the students. During Avi's senior year, he submitted an entry to the playwriting contest. One judge wrote on the manuscript, "This person obviously is not an English-speaking person, but he is making great strides in learning the language and should be encouraged."

After graduating from the University of Wisconsin, Avi stayed on for one more year to do graduate work in playwriting. Undaunted by the judge's response to his previous entry in the student playwriting contest, Avi submitted another play the next year. Drawing on his interest in history, Avi wrote a comedy about the American Revolution entitled *A Little Rebellion*. With this submission, he won the contest. His play was published in two different magazines, and the university staged a production of it. At age twenty-two, Avi was a produced playwright. What next?

Chapter 9
Making a Living,
Making a Life

In 1960, after five years in Wisconsin, Avi decided to continue his writing career in San Francisco. He accepted a job as resident playwright at the World Theater there and moved into the North Beach area. At the time, San Francisco was home to many writers of the "beat" generation. In the 1950s, these writers and artists scorned traditional middle-class American values and sought enlightenment through Zen Buddhism and other non-Western religions. They were the rebels of their day.

In spite of Avi's connection to the art world in San Francisco, he was unaware of the beat generation writers while he was there. His theater work absorbed all of his time and attention.

Life in the theater world is a precarious existence. While many people write plays, few are able to get their plays produced. Staging a play takes a huge financial investment well before the play starts making money. A theater must be rented, actors must be paid while they rehearse, sets must be built, and advertisements need to be run in newspapers. Playwrights, no matter how talented, have to be able to convince people to invest large sums of money in their work. To get a play produced on the stage takes a combination of talent, connections to the right people, and pure luck.

In San Francisco, Avi wasn't able to put that combination together. As resident playwright for the World Theater, it was his job to write plays, and he did. Although the theater managers planned to produce one of the plays, ultimately they decided against it. After a year in California, feeling discouraged about his prospects, Avi returned to New York City. He settled in the borough of Manhattan, home of the most famous theater district in the United States—Broadway.

In New York, Avi continued to write, but now he had to find a way to make a living while he tried to get his plays produced. At first, he took any job he could find. He printed signs, sometimes with spelling mistakes. Using the skills he had learned as a boy in Harry Oncher's shop, he did carpentry. He worked as a drama coach, helping actors improve their skills. None of the jobs satisfied him, but they paid the bills while he wrote.

While working as a drama coach at a YMHA (Young Men's Hebrew Association) in the Bronx, Avi began to date the dance coach, a woman named Joan Gainer. After a while, the two of them began to think about marriage. Joan was a modern ballet dancer with an income just as uncertain as Avi's. Clearly, if they were going to plan a future together, one of them would have to have a steady job. Avi started looking around for work.

One day he wandered into the sprawling building on West 42nd Street that houses the New York Public Library. The library needed a clerk to work in its theater collection. What better job for a part-time playwright who loved books and needed a steady job!

Shortly after starting his job at the library, Avi learned some exciting news. In about three years, the library was going to move its performing arts collection twenty blocks north to Lincoln Center, a brand-new complex of buildings devoted to the performing arts. When the library moved the collection to Lincoln Center, a larger staff would be needed. Avi saw possibilities for career advancement, but he knew that when the staff expanded, the better jobs would go to people who had college degrees in library science. That week, he enrolled in library science courses at Columbia University. Attending school at night while he worked during the day, Avi eventually got a master's degree in library science.

Even though Avi was working and going to school, he continued to write plays. When he first returned to New

York, a backer had expressed interest in producing one of his plays on Broadway and in London. This backer encouraged Avi to get a literary agent, someone to represent him in negotiations with people who might want to buy his written work. Avi signed with a well-known literary agency. Unfortunately, even with an agent to represent him, Avi was not able to get the play produced. Having an agent, however, made Avi think of himself as a professional writer and as a part of the New York literary world, even though he had not yet earned a cent from his writing.

For the next three or four years, Avi spent much of his spare time writing plays, "a trunkful," he now says, "but ninety-nine percent of them weren't any good." An older friend, seeing Avi struggle with his plays, suggested that he write novels, that perhaps playwriting was too difficult for him. Eventually Avi wrote a couple of short novels for adults, similar to the kinds of books he now writes for children. The friend read them and thought well of them. He put Avi in touch with another literary agency, which specialized in fiction. As a courtesy to Avi's friend, the head of the agency read Avi's novels and tried to sell them to a publisher, without any luck.

On November 1, 1963, Avi and Joan Gainer married at a private ceremony in a Unitarian church in Brooklyn. They had not told their parents about the wedding beforehand. After the ceremony, they hailed a cab and went to Avi's parents' home to announce the marriage. In 1966, their first child, a boy they named Shaun, was born. Avi was delighted with the baby and fascinated with his new role as father.

With a wife and baby to provide for, Avi continued to look for ways to supplement his librarian's salary. He still liked to draw. For some time, he had been designing humorous greeting cards to send to friends. One of his friends suggested that Avi create a series of greeting cards to sell.

The greeting cards themselves were completely unsuccessful, but another friend of Avi's saw them, liked them, and asked Avi to illustrate a children's book she was writing. Avi really didn't want to do this. He considered himself a writer, not an artist. Still, he agreed to help out his friend. When his friend tried to sell the finished book to a publishing company, the editor wasn't interested in the story, but she loved the pictures. She asked the writer, "Who is this artist? We'd like to sign him up to illustrate a book."

Avi met with the editor and explained that he was not an illustrator, that in fact he was a writer. "Fine," she said, "then write a book and illustrate it."

Avi, Joan, and two-year-old Shaun were about to leave for England. Avi was to work in a library in England for a year while an English librarian came to New York and did his job. He didn't really have time to write a book before they left, but this seemed too good an opportunity to pass up.

In the few weeks remaining before their trip, Avi sat down and wrote a children's book. It was based on a game that he and Shaun played. Shaun would say, "Tell me a story." Avi would reply, "What do you want a story about?" Shaun would answer, "Tell me a story about a glass of water." Or maybe Shaun would say "a black crayon" or "a subway ride." Avi took all of the stories he could remember telling Shaun and wrote them down. Then he gave the book to his agent and left for England.

In 1968, while Avi and his family were in England, Joan gave birth to their second child, Kevin. Shaun's birth had been very traditional, with Avi waiting outside the delivery room until the excitement was over. Much to Avi's delight, he was allowed to stay in the delivery room with Joan and to assist at Kevin's birth. It was a thrilling experience for him.

In England, Avi and his family sometimes visited with Avi's brother, Henry, who was living there with his wife and two children. Henry was busy doing scientific research. Mostly, the two families got together for dinner and conversation.

At the time, Henry decided to grow a beard and mustache, something his "little brother" had done years before. On seeing Henry's new facial hair, Avi informed him that it looked terrible and that he should shave it off. Henry said he would if Avi would shave his beard and mustache, too. Avi agreed. Neither Joan nor Shaun had ever seen Avi without a beard and mustache. Both of them took one look at the shorn Avi and burst into tears. To appease his family, Avi soon sported a new mustache and beard.

The year they lived in England, Avi and his family took a vacation in Spain, choosing that country because it was relatively easy to get there from England. A ferry from Plymouth delivered them and their car to Spain.

What were the highlights of the trip for Avi? Today what he remembers is that the car kept breaking down and that he carried Kevin everywhere on his back. Because of the baby's great smile, they made friends wherever they went.

While Avi was in England, his agent took his collection of children's stories to the editor who had expressed interest in Avi's illustrations. She wasn't interested in publishing the book, but after several more attempts to sell the book, the agent found a publishing company that was interested. Ironically, the new publisher didn't want Avi to illustrate the book and used another artist instead. In 1970, *Things That Sometimes Happen*, subtitled *Thirty Very Short Stories for Very Young Readers*, was released. Avi dedicated the book to Shaun, who had inspired the stories.

Before the book was published, Avi's agent asked him how he wanted his name to appear on the book. Avi replied, "Oh, just say Avi." So, from the very beginning of his publishing career, he has been called simply "Avi."

From the time Avi had announced his intention to become a writer in his diary until *Things That Sometimes Happen* was published in 1970, fifteen years had passed. Since then, Avi has published more than thirty books for young people.

When *Things That Sometimes Happen* was published, Avi was writing his third novel for adults. Right away, he stopped working on it. All three of his adult novels remain unpublished. Once he turned his attention to writing for young people, he never returned to writing adult novels or plays.

Years of writing plays, however, must have had an effect on Avi's writing. His books contain lots of dialogue and have the same kind of dramatic structure as plays. Some have actually been produced as plays. Others—namely, *Wolf Rider*; *City of Light, City of Dark*; *Sometimes I Think I Hear My Name*; and *The True Confessions of Charlotte Doyle*—have been optioned by film producers. Being optioned doesn't guarantee that the books will ever be made into films, but it does show that film producers recognize the dramatic potential of Avi's books.

When Avi and his family returned to the United States from England, they settled in Brooklyn. Avi went back to work at the New York Public Library at Lincoln Center. While his salary of eleven thousand dollars a year had been enough when he was paying sixty-two dollars a month for rent, it was becoming increasingly more difficult to support a wife and two children on that sum. He needed a job that would pay more.

In 1970, he found it when he was offered a job as librarian at Trenton State College in Trenton, New Jersey. That year, Avi and his family moved to New Jersey, and Avi started a job that would last seventeen years. Later he also taught classes in children's literature at the college.

Although he was always busy with a full-time job and his writing, Avi loved being a parent and was very much involved in his children's lives. As one would expect of a librarian and writer, he especially loved reading to Shaun and Kevin. He read them his own books, of course, but he also read them books by many other authors. Avi says he got as much out of the reading as his children did. It broadened his knowledge of books. It gave him an aware-ness of the many different kinds of children's books there are. It let him see firsthand what children enjoy in books. Today Avi says, "My children gave me my profession." Not that he ever wrote about Shaun and Kevin or things that they did as children, but rather his children allowed him to enter into the world of childhood, which inspires his writing even today, long after Kevin and Shaun have left childhood behind.

What was it like having an author for a father? Avi says his children led very normal lives. In fact, they some-times complain jokingly that their parents were too nice and didn't make any problems for them. There was noth-ing to struggle against.

The family did the everyday kinds of things that most families do. They went to the movies and visited friends. During the school year, the focus was on school activities. Occasionally during the summer, the four of them would join Avi's brother and his family at the house on Shelter Island.

While he was teaching classes in children's literature at Trenton, Avi began to collect children's books, both old and current ones. Avi had great fun looking for books in used bookstores or at yard sales. Most of the ones he bought cost no more than a dime or a quarter. Some were first editions. The collection, which eventually numbered three thousand books, reflected Avi's interest in history. He bought a wide variety of books because he wanted to see where his books fit into the whole spectrum of Ameri-can books for children.

In 1976, while he was still working at Trenton State, Avi and his family moved from New Jersey to New Hope, Pennsylvania. Although the move took them across a state line and to the other side of the Delaware River, the new house was actually only about a mile from the old one. They had moved not for a change of scenery, but because their house in New Jersey had become too small for two adults and two growing boys. Also, Joan had given up dancing and had become a weaver. She needed studio space in their home.

As Avi wrote more and more children's books, he began to travel around the country to speak in schools and libraries about his books and about writing. Avi enjoyed the opportunity to build a larger audience for his books and to hear from his readers firsthand. Fortunately, he had flexibility in his librarian's job. He might have to work fifteen hours a day for a while, but then he could take off for a few days to travel around promoting his books.

Still, he was working several jobs at the same time—full-time librarian, full-time writer, and full-time parent. There wasn't enough of him to go around. Something had to give. It was his marriage. During his years of working day and night, Avi and his wife had grown apart. In 1982, they separated and eventually divorced. Soon after that, Shaun went off to college. Kevin lived with Joan while he finished high school. Avi stayed in the same neighborhood so he could be close to his son.

It seems that Avi's sister, Emily, has a streak of match-maker in her. Years earlier, she had introduced her brother

Henry to his wife. After Avi's divorce, Emily thought of a college friend, Coppélia Kahn, who had also recently divorced. Maybe she and Avi would enjoy each other's company, thought Emily. As it turned out, they did. Soon they were making plans to get married.

Coppélia Kahn, who has a son named Gabriel, taught literature at Wesleyan College in Connecticut. Avi was still living in Pennsylvania, but he applied for and got a job as a librarian in Connecticut. Before he could move and start the job in Connecticut, Coppélia was offered a professorship at Brown University in Providence, Rhode Island. Avi turned down the job in Connecticut, but instead of looking for a job as a librarian in Rhode Island, he decided it was time to see if he could support himself solely by his writing. In 1987, after seventeen years as a college librarian, he left his job at Trenton State and moved to Providence to become a full-time writer.

Avi's paternal grandparents (front) and his great-uncle

Avi's parents, Joseph and Helen Wortis, in 1959

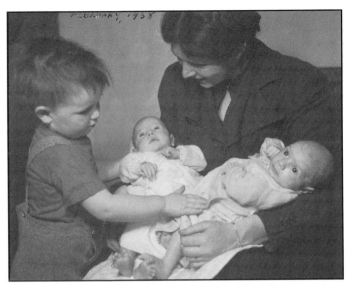

*Avi's mother, Helen, with Henry and twins Emily and
Avi at age two months*

*Helen and Joseph with
Henry, Avi, and Emily
(Avi and Emily are six
months old.)*

Emily at age 11 months

Avi at age 11 months

Joseph and Helen with Emily, Henry, and Avi

A gathering of Avi's family in 1940 (from left to right): Avi's aunts, Beadie (top) and Rosellen; Beadie's son Alan; Avi's grandmother and grandfather; Henry, Avi, Joseph, and Emily

Avi (at 12 months) with his father, older brother Henry, and Chungo, the family dog

Avi at 18 months

Avi at the beach in August of 1940

Avi at age four

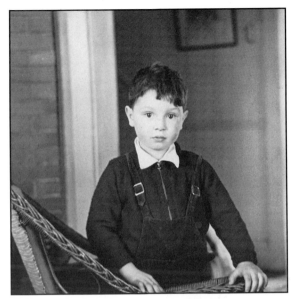

Avi at age five

Avi and Emily at a neighborhood birthday party. Avi is in the middle of the second row.

Avi and Emily at age five

Avi at the time of his high school graduation

Avi's high school soccer team. Avi is third from the left in the front row.

Avi at his parents' home in 1957

Avi's son, Shaun,
at 12 months

Avi's son, Kevin, at
three years of age

Avi in 1990

Avi at home in 1992

Avi at his home in Providence

Chapter 10
Occupation: Writer

Ask any author who writes for young people what question readers most often ask, and the answer is almost always, "Where do you get your ideas?" Avi has given much thought to this question. The answer, he says, is complicated. For one thing, he is convinced that when people ask that question, they are not really asking where he got the idea for a specific book. Rather, they are asking themselves, without really knowing it, why *they* don't have ideas for books. The simple answer is that most people don't think about books all the time as Avi does.

Avi says it's especially hard for today's young people to get ideas for stories because they watch so much television. Television viewers don't see their own lives reflected in the plots of most television shows. Because of this, they fail to recognize the meaning in their own lives and, therefore, don't convert their own experiences into stories.

When Avi visits schools he tries to show students that they do have ideas for stories and, furthermore, that they can train themselves to have ideas. For example, he might start with something very simple, like the name of the school. Who is the school named after? Why is it named after that person? Did everyone agree that it should be named after that person, or was there some conflict? Two hundred years ago, what was happening where the school stands now? Avi asks this last question because, he says, stories have to do with change, and if you don't notice that things change, then you can't think of stories.

As for himself, Avi says he gets ideas for stories all the time. He thinks in stories. In fact, says Avi, he uses only a fraction of the stories he thinks about. The rest he forgets. "I can make up a story about anything," Avi boasts. Then he humbly admits, "That doesn't mean they are all good. But if I have the basis for a story, I can make it good if I choose to."

More specifically, Avi says that an idea for a book usually doesn't come in one flash of inspiration. Rather, a story idea comes to him in bits and pieces—from random thoughts, chance observations, and overheard remarks. He traces his book *Sometimes I Think I Hear My Name*, for example, to these roots: the living situation of a young person he knew, his wife's remark about the way some other young people were living, a writer friend's statement about a place, another friend's remark about a parent, and a quotation from the mystery writer Ross MacDonald, who said "Most fiction is shaped by geography and permeated by autobiography, even when it is trying not to be."

These disjointed thoughts and observations linked together to form an idea for a story. How did the linking happen? Avi can't say for sure, but as a reader and writer, he has taught himself to think about people and events in terms of plots—plots that have locations, beginnings, conflicts, and endings.

For many years, Avi made a very brief outline for each book, a list of no more than twenty main events that would take place in the book. Now he makes this kind of outline in his head rather than on paper.

At the outlining stage, Avi lets the story rattle around in his mind before putting a word on paper. This thinking stage may go on for months or even years. As he thinks, Avi may make changes in his mental outline. At this point, he thinks only about events rather than characters or settings. He tries hard not to think about what he wants the story to mean. The meaning, he believes, will come out of the story.

Once Avi has the idea for a story, he must often spend time researching, especially if the book is set in an earlier historical period. His many years as a librarian taught him how to research efficiently. To be sure he captures the details of historical settings, Avi even browses through books of costumes and photographs of the period he's writing about.

When Avi needs to experience a place firsthand, he does research on location. While he was writing *The Barn*, set in the Oregon Territory in 1855, he went to live in Oregon. For *The True Confessions of Charlotte Doyle*, most of which takes place on a ship in 1832, he was able to do research closer to home by visiting old ships in museums along the Rhode Island and Connecticut waterfront. For a book he was working on in 1995, a long historical novel, Avi visited Ireland and then spent some time in Lowell, Massachusetts.

When Avi starts writing, he spends a lot of time on the opening page of a book. Here is where a reader decides whether to continue or not, and Avi works hard to set the tone, the mood, and the rhythm he wants the book to have. After page one, it's just a matter of writing what comes next. Actually, for Avi, that is stating the case too simply. In fact, Avi is never exactly sure where a book is headed. For example, when he started *The History of Helpless Harry*, he planned to write a tragedy about a boy driven to evil by his own fearfulness. After a suggestion by Avi's agent, which resulted in several rewrites, the story turned out to be an uproarious comedy with a hero who, despite his misguided ways, wins the hearts of readers by his courageous stand against evil.

When he gets to the writing stage, Avi works on a computer. He starts on page one and writes a sentence. Then he rewrites the sentence. Finishing a paragraph, he rewrites the paragraph. At the end of a page, he rewrites the page. When he gets to page forty, he goes back and rewrites page one. To revise, he prints out what he wants to work on, makes his changes on the paper copy, inputs the changes into the computer, and then destroys all previous versions of the manuscript.

"Endlessly, endlessly rewriting" is how Avi describes his process. He rewrites all of his books forty or fifty times. Because of his dysgraphia, he may read a sentence many times without catching obvious mistakes in it. For example, he may write *followed* when he meant to write *foolish*. The mistake may be in the manuscript for a year before he notices it.

To find errors, sometimes Avi reads his work aloud. This seems to focus his eyes in a slightly different way and lets him see mistakes he wouldn't normally notice. He has developed other tricks for catching errors. For example, he may change the margins to fool his eyes into seeing things differently.

Avi revises for both content and style. In other words, he sometimes changes both the story and the words he uses to tell the story. "Writing is hard for me," he says. "I love it, but I'm not a natural writer. I don't know who is. I think writing is hard for everyone."

Avi has described himself as a slow writer who works quickly. His work on a book is divided into two phases. The first phase is fast and intense. At the end, he has a completed rough draft—very rough. In fact, Avi has said that he wouldn't show one of his first drafts to his cat. The second phase is long and slow, as he rereads and rewrites.

Throughout the revision process, Avi looks for suggestions from trusted readers. He always listens carefully to what his agent and his editor have to say. Rarely do they bring up something he hasn't already been thinking about, but their concerns are enough to send him back to the computer for another rewrite.

No matter how good agents and editors are, they are not the main audience for whom Avi writes. To get a reaction from his future readers, Avi likes to read a book-in-the-making to young people. He has read several of his manuscripts in their entirety to students at Moses Brown School in Providence. What kind of criticism does he get from students? Well, they don't throw rotten tomatoes at him or hiss and boo. "I'm a good reader and a nice person, so it's all stacked in my favor," says Avi, "but you can hear the dead spots and the restlessness." When he senses that restlessness, Avi knows that he has to go back to the computer for some more rewriting.

Avi realizes that there is no such thing as a perfect book. How, then, does he decide when he is finished with a book? Three things can cause him to stop rewriting. One, and this rarely happens, he becomes truly exhausted and simply can't face the manuscript anymore. Two, he realizes that the changes he is making are minor, that he could be shifting words around for the next hundred years and not make the book significantly better. Three, the editor says, "Stop! We've got to get this thing to press."

From then on, the book is in the hands of the publishing company. Often Avi works with his editors to choose illustrators for his books, but he always trusts the editor's final decision. When a book is finally set in type, Avi reads the typeset book one last time before it goes to the printer.

Once the book is at the printer, Avi waits for the finished copies—and the reviews. For a while, Avi used to write reviews of other authors' books. Now he doesn't do that. "I have a lot of problems with book reviews," he says. Avi thinks that reviewers of children's books have enormous power in determining which books sell, and yet some reviewers don't do a very good job. Often, the reviewer doesn't look at the book as a work of literature, focusing instead on how it will fit into a school curriculum. Many reviews are no more than a summary of the book with a one-sentence approval or disapproval. Still, Avi does read the reviews of his books. Sometimes he gets upset and angry about them. "Sometimes I think I shouldn't read them, but I do," he admits.

Chapter 11
Talking About Writing

Avi not only loves to write, he loves to talk about writing, too. He thinks a lot about why he does it and how he does it. Avi enjoys sharing his thoughts with others.

Why he writes is rooted in the experiences of his past and his hopes for the future. From an early age, Avi was entertained by the stories family members told. Now he sees stories in a different light. They are entertainment, but they are also maps. Avi explains his comparison between stories and maps in this way. Before European settlers arrived in Australia, that land's nomadic people had an oral literature rather than a written one. The characters in their stories traveled to and from various locations. The stories were actually maps that helped the people find their way around the stark and beautiful interior of the continent. To Avi, all stories are maps—maps for life's journey. He writes because he wants to show young people some difficulties they may experience and some ways to proceed on their journeys.

Avi's desire to make story maps comes from his respect for young people. He has said that most young people are as emotionally complex as adults. Some perhaps are more complex. He's also convinced that today's young people are aware of the harsh realities of life. Therefore, he never tries to simplify complicated situations. Although Avi writes a tight, fast-paced, compelling story that has the reader racing to the end, he aims to create characters and situations that readers will remember long after they have finished the book.

Avi also writes out of the crusading spirit he learned from his family and embraced as his own. He believes the world can be a better place and wants to be part of making it better. Through children's literature, Avi sees a way of promoting such powerful, positive values as sharing, nonviolence, cooperation, and the ability to love. As he sees it, these values are not represented in many adult books.

Avi believes that the field of children's literature is not treated seriously. He feels that authors and editors of children's books and children's librarians are not paid well because, "in a basic sense, contemporary children's literature is critical of the adult world in which it exists."[1]

In a 1987 magazine article, Avi wrote, "If we—in the world of children's literature—can help the young . . . maintain their ideals and values, those with which you and I identify ourselves, help them demand—and win—justice, we've added something good to the world."[2]

Avi gets lots of letters from young people who appreciate his honest view of life. These readers like the hard questions he tackles, the ironies he exposes, the dilemmas he refuses to resolve for them. Avi treasures responses from readers. He believes the best compliment he ever received was a letter from a reader who wrote, "Thank you for putting another book in the world." Reactions like this give Avi the *why* of his writing.

Avi also willingly shares *how* he came to write his books. At first, he wrote picture books at his sons' reading levels. As his sons grew up and their reading tastes changed, Avi kept writing, but a few years went by when he didn't publish any books. One time he sold a manuscript to a publishing company, but the book was never published because the company went out of business. One of those early manuscripts was published in 1994 as *The Bird, the Frog, and the Light*. Another of his unpublished stories became the Simon part of his 1995 collection of three fairy tales, *Tom, Babette, & Simon*.

In 1975, Avi wrote *No More Magic*, his first novel for young people. He was pleased with it, and so was the publisher. From that point on, Avi committed himself to writing novels for young people.

Actually, Avi sees novels for young people as novellas, a form halfway between a short story and a full-length novel. The novella is his favorite form—to read and to write. "I love the book you can swallow in one long drink," he says. Writing novellas gives him a sense of greater control over the events in a book. He can read what he has written many times over as he works on the book and can get an overall picture of what he has created so far. Often when he reads his manuscript over, he sees things he wants to change.

In spite of his comfort with the novella form, Avi tackled a very different kind of book in the mid-1990s. He decided to write a Victorian novel for young people. "Victorian" refers to the last half of the nineteenth century, the period when Queen Victoria ruled Britain. Victorian novels are usually several hundred pages long and have many characters and very complicated plots. In fact, Avi's Victorian novel, entitled *Beyond the Western Sea*, is comprised of two books. Victorian novels are about as different as they can be from novellas. Avi's decision to write one shows how committed he is to trying out new ideas in his writing.

Besides trying out different forms, Avi loves to experiment with different ways of telling stories. Many of his books are historical fiction set in various periods of United States history. *Encounter at Easton*, for example, takes place before the American Revolution, *The Fighting Ground* covers one day during the revolution, and *Smugglers' Island* is set during the 1930s.

To Avi, history is not dull, dry facts but absorbing stories of real people. If he is driving along a road and sees a historic marker, he almost always stops to read it and imagine what happened there. When he looks at a battlefield, with just a little imagination, he can see the events that unfolded there. He considers the little details of history more important than who won or lost the battle. To make this point during an interview, Avi mentioned to the interviewer that during the Battle of Bunker Hill in the American Revolution, Dr. Warren, the leader of the American troops, was killed. His body was so disfigured that he could only be identified by his teeth. Paul Revere made the identification. Details like that reveal the true horrors of war to Avi.

Although Avi enjoys writing historical fiction, he has also written books about contemporary young people, mystery stories, suspense novels, and fantasy. He has even written a comic-book novel. Some of his books combine several different styles. *Something Upstairs*, for example, is a ghost story, but it also has elements of history and science fiction.

Collaborating with an artist on his comic-book novel, *City of Light, City of Dark*, was probably Avi's most unusual writing experience. First Avi wrote a novel. Then he cut out everything but the essential dialogue, or spoken words. He gave the dialogue to the artist, Brian Floca. Floca was a student of well-known illustrator David Macaulay. He had the added advantage of living around the corner from Avi. Floca did a layout and sketches loosely based on the dialogue Avi gave him. When Avi saw the sketches, he threw out everything he had written up to that point and wrote a brand new work that corresponded to the artist's layout. It seems like a lot of work for one book, but it was also a lot of fun, according to Avi.

Because Avi tries so many different forms and styles, readers who like one of his books aren't always interested in his others. Those who love his historical fiction, for example, may not want to read a suspense story. Readers frequently request that Avi write sequels to his books. Avi has a theory about series books. He thinks they are really family books. Kids like them because they create a sense of family, and family is very important to young people.

So far, Avi has only written two sequels. His historical novel *Encounter at Easton* picks up the story where *Night Journeys* leaves off. After writing these two books, Avi did something interesting. An earlier book, *Captain Grey*, was about to be reprinted. He changed the story slightly so that it could be connected to *Night Journeys* and *Encounter at Easton*. In the second edition of *Captain Grey*, the title character is the boy in *Encounter at Easton* grown to adulthood.

Avi also wrote a sequel to *S.O.R. Losers*, his comic contemporary novel about a misfit soccer team. *Romeo and Juliet—Together (and Alive!) at Last* portrays the same group of oddballs coming together to put on a hilarious version of the Shakespeare classic. The sole purpose of the play is to cast one of their shy friends as Romeo and the girl he has a crush on as Juliet.

For a writer who has written so many books, it's surprising that Avi hasn't drawn more from his own life. Yet very few of his novels are autobiographical. *S.O.R. Losers* is based on his high school soccer team, but only loosely. *"Who Was That Masked Man, Anyway?"* portrays Avi's boyhood fascination with radio programs and the workings of his vivid imagination. Avi admits, however, that the boldly adventurous main character is not what he was like, but rather what he wished he were like at the time.

Avi's only other autobiographical novel is *Wolf Rider*, a chilling tale of suspense written for older readers. In the book, the fifteen-year-old narrator receives an anonymous phone call from a man claiming to have killed a woman, whom he names and describes. This actually happened to Avi when he lived in New Jersey. One night he received a random, anonymous call from someone claiming to have killed a woman. Avi kept the caller talking for forty-five minutes while the police tried, unsuccessfully, to trace the call. The police then told Avi to forget about the incident. He had done all he could. Naturally, Avi couldn't forget it. He found the woman's name in the phone book and called her to warn her. She was a police officer, and Avi's anonymous caller had described her accurately. Avi felt this woman had reason to be concerned, but he had been told by the police not to get involved. Later, he told a reporter that he felt he should call the woman again to express his concern. The reporter warned him, "Don't do it. The police will think that you were the caller, that it was a hoax." Avi took the reporter's advice, but the whole incident haunted him, and he wrote *Wolf Rider* to try to put the incident behind him.

Even though he calls only three of his books autobiographical, bits and pieces of Avi's life show up in several of his novels. Many of the fathers in his books resemble his father. Avi uses the father in *Poppy*, for example, to poke fun at some of his father's traits. Avi's cousin, Michael, who lived around the corner from Avi when they were growing up, turns up as Mario in *"Who Was That Masked Man, Anyway?"* and under his own last name in *S.O.R. Losers* and *Romeo and Juliet—Together (and Alive!) at Last*.

Avi definitely draws on his own experiences for the settings of his books. *A Place Called Ugly* was inspired by Shelter Island. *No More Magic* takes place in the town in New Jersey where he lived for many years. *Night Journeys* and *Encounter at Easton* are set in the area around New Hope, Pennsylvania, where he moved when he left New Jersey. *Devil's Race* features an area in Pennsylvania where Avi used to go camping as an adult. The three books he wrote just after moving to Providence, Rhode Island—*Something Upstairs*, *The Man Who Was Poe*, and *The True Confessions of Charlotte Doyle*—were all inspired by Providence. The setting for *Blue Heron* is a vacation cottage in Massachusetts that Avi and Coppélia share with another person.

Having written so many books, does Avi have any favorites? He answers that question differently at different times. Sometimes he says his next book is his favorite. Other times, he'll admit that certain books are close to his heart. *City of Light, City of Dark*, his comic-book novel, was "wonderful fun to do." He calls *"Who Was That Masked Man, Anyway?"* his funniest book. He reserves his highest praise for *The Barn*, a novella that takes place in the Oregon Territory in 1855. Avi calls this book "emotionally satisfying" and "as close to a perfect book as I've ever written. It's all there and very compact."

Chapter 12
The Ideas Behind the Books

Avi is first and foremost a storyteller. When he writes, he wants to create a plot that will keep readers asking, "And then what happened?" Behind every exciting story, however, are ideas for readers to think about. Even though Avi's stories are all very different, the same themes or ideas come up again and again. These are ideas that Avi thinks about a lot.

Many of Avi's main characters are orphans, don't live with their parents, or have parents who are emotionally distant, much as Avi's own father was. Often the main characters' parents disappoint them in some important way. Many of his characters rebel against authority because they live in an adult world that is unjust, violent, or uncaring. These characters must often face life alone and alienated from the world in which they live. Other characters are set apart from the adult world by their belief in magic or the supernatural. Whether an Avi book is historical fiction, fantasy, mystery, suspense, or realistic contemporary fiction, it usually explores at least one of these ideas. Many of his books cover more than one of these themes.

The theme of magic shows up in Avi's earliest books and in others written more than twenty years later. In Avi's books, magic can be a way for a young person to escape from the adult world, to try to control it, or to try to understand it.

Many of the stories in Avi's first book, *Things That Sometimes Happen,* take place in the kind of innocent, magical world where a glass of water can talk to an elephant. Although grown-ups inhabit this world, they don't always understand how remarkable it is. In one story, a little boy meets a fish who takes him underwater to see where fish live. There, the little boy chats and shares his cookies with several friendly fish. When he gets home, his Papa asks him what he has been doing, and the little boy answers, "I went to feed the fishes in the water." "What a nice thing to do," replies the dad, who assumes that his son has been feeding conventional fish from the edge of a pond. Like many of the fathers in Avi's books, this one just doesn't live in the same kind of world as his child.

Another father who doesn't see the magic in life turns up in Avi's first novel, *No More Magic*. Chris believes that magical events have caused the disappearance of his bike and his friend's Halloween costume. His dad, a college librarian (as Avi was at the time he wrote the book), exasperates Chris by insisting on a logical approach to solving the mysteries. "Get your questions right before you get your answers wrong," he repeatedly advises Chris. When the mysteries are finally solved, the adults maintain that there was a logical explanation for the disappearances. "There's no more magic," claims Chris's dad, and readers almost have to agree with him. Still, Chris has the last word. When his Green Lantern ring begins to glow mysteriously, Chris asserts, "And he says there's no more magic. Maybe. Maybe not." Perhaps Chris's father is right about magic, but Avi makes it clear that Chris is the one who is having more fun.

Years later, Avi wrote *Blue Heron*, another novel about a parent and child who have different views on magic. Maggie, whose parents are divorced, goes to visit her father every summer. Maggie thinks that magic should keep things the same, not change them. One summer, she wishes for her father to be the same as always, but the magic doesn't work. There are many changes. Her father and his second wife have a new baby, and her father is strangely tense and uncommunicative. To escape the tension at the vacation cottage, Maggie spends a lot of time watching a blue heron at the nearby lake, fascinated by the creature's beauty and grace. Eventually, she becomes aware that someone else is also watching the heron, someone who seems to want to harm it. During the summer, Maggie reaches out both to her father and to the heron's stalker. While she manages to push through the stalker's pain and reach the person behind it, she cannot completely break through the barrier her father has erected. Still, she finally learns what is troubling him, and this helps her realize that, despite the tension, he does love her. Near the end of the book, Maggie's father tells her to forget magic. It doesn't work. But through his story, Avi shows that both Maggie and her father are wrong. There is a special magic—both in nature and in the connections between people. In *Blue Heron* this magic works, even if it doesn't keep things from changing.

Although the characters in *No More Magic* and *Blue Heron* talk about magic and believe in it, nothing out of the ordinary happens in either book. In some of Avi's other books, however, certain events cannot be explained by anything but magic. Readers must put aside their disbelief and enter into worlds created by Avi's imagination. *Bright Shadow*, for example, is a fantasy that takes place in an imaginary time and place. When a dying wizard gives Morwenna the last five wishes in the kingdom, she must decide how to use them. Morwenna's mother says magic is hope and wishes are dreams. With wishes, things can change; without them things stay the same. Much in the kingdom needs to be changed, but Morwenna learns that, even with wishes, there is a price to pay for change.

Devil's Race and *Something Upstairs* are tales of the supernatural. In them, Avi uses the theme of magic to show how the main characters grow and change when they confront evil. In *Devil's Run*, evil takes the form of the ghost of the main character's great-great-great-great-grandfather, who was hanged in 1854 for being a demon. After visiting his ancestor's grave, sixteen-year-old John Proud begins to feel that he has supernatural powers. Exercising the powers, however, brings only tragedy. John attempts to learn more about the forces that seem to be controlling him by backpacking into the wilderness, which represents not only a physical struggle but also an emotional one. What he faces in the wilderness makes him a stronger person in the end.

Something Upstairs is a ghost story with a science fiction twist. The ghost is a young slave who was murdered in 1800. When he appears in the old Providence house that Kenny Huldorf has recently moved to, he convinces Kenny to travel back in time with him to find his murderer. Whether Kenny will be able to return to the present depends solely on his own cleverness at outwitting the evil murderer. This suspenseful ghost story is more than an adventure tale. Its real subject is the responsibility one human being feels for the well-being of another. Kenny risks his life to aid the ghost because he sees a situation that is wrong and must be righted.

Many of Avi's characters find themselves in the same situation as Kenny Huldorf. Faced with injustice or a situation that just seems wrong to them, they choose to fight the system, rather than accept it. These characters reflect the ideals that Avi learned from his family: that all people have a right to be treated fairly and that it is important to stand up for this right and to help others stand up for their rights. Avi explores this theme in many books—historical and modern, humorous and serious.

In one of his early historical novels, *Night Journeys*, set in 1768, orphaned teenager Peter York is taken in by a Quaker family. Peter longs to escape from the strict life of his new family. He sees a chance when a reward is offered for the capture of two runaway indentured servants. If Peter can earn the reward, he will be able to buy back his horse and escape. It seems simple, but when he learns the ages of the runaways and why they were forced into servitude, Peter begins to question whether or not he is doing the right thing. Is his own freedom more important than that of two mistreated children? What is the right thing to do? These are the hard questions Peter must face.

Smugglers' Island is another of Avi's historical novels that develops the theme of young people's fight for justice. The story takes place in 1932 during the Prohibition Era, when alcohol could not be sold legally anywhere in the United States. Illegal liquor, however, was made available by smugglers. In this novel, one group of bootleggers has chosen Lucker's Island as its base of operation. Taking liquor from ships twelve miles offshore, they store it on the island and then transport it to the mainland for sale. Lucker's Island is also home to some forty people, all of them impoverished by the Great Depression and all of them terrified to defy the smugglers. All but one, that is. Twelve-year-old Shadrach Flaherty despises the smugglers. He hates what they have done to his parents and the other adults of the island, making them cower behind closed doors while the bootleggers unload illegal liquor at the dock. Shadrach vows to bring the smugglers to justice. Before he can do so, however, he has to decide which of the two newcomers to the island he can trust to help him. Making the wrong choice could endanger his life. Shadrach has to fight not only the smugglers but also the timidity of the adults around him. This is a common theme in Avi's books.

Avi used humor to explore the theme of young people standing up for their beliefs in *S.O.R. Losers*, a novel based on his high school soccer team, which lost every game for two years straight. The fictional South Orange River (S.O.R.) Middle School is famed for its championship-winning teams. There's even a school rule: everyone must play one sport a year. But Ed Sitrow and his buddies couldn't care less about sports. They are poets and artists and musicians and math whizzes, but not athletes. Against their will, they are made into a soccer team with a coach as incompetent as they are. As the team loses game after game by huge scores, the school builds to a frenzy of support for them. Everybody at S.O.R. Middle School wants this soccer team to win, everybody but the members of the team themselves. They don't particularly care. In the end, they stand up for their right to be terrible at soccer in their own unique way. As in so many of Avi's books, it's the young people who have to show adults the way.

Trying to show adults the way can cause difficulties for young people, and several of Avi's books explore strained relationships between young people and their parents. *No More Magic*, *Blue Heron*, and *Smugglers' Island* all involve the main characters in struggles with their parents. Even Avi's two historical farces, *The History of Helpless Harry* and *Emily Upham's Revenge*, despite their comic tone, have characters who reject their parents' view of things.

Emily Upham's Revenge: A Massachusetts Adventure details the adventures of the prim and proper, but thoroughly determined, Emily Upham. When Emily's banker father goes bankrupt, Emily is sent to live with her prosperous uncle. Emily never reaches her uncle's house, but through the series of misadventures that prevent her from getting there, she begins to realize what a corrupting force money is in her family's life. Emily would never dream of raising her voice to a grown-up, but in her own unique way she wreaks a terrible, though comic, revenge on her father and uncle for their preoccupation with money. There is lots of fun in *Emily Upham's Revenge*, but there is also a serious tale about adults who misjudge the determination and character of young people and who pay dearly for their misjudgments.

The History of Helpless Harry is the story of little Horatio Stockton Edgeworth, the only child of overprotective parents. Despite their attachment to Harry, Mr. and Mrs. Edgeworth plan a journey without him. Left in the care of Miss Annie Towbridge, Harry immediately decides that she is bent on stealing his father's money box. The arrival on the scene of Mr. Pym, to whom Annie is secretly married, and a con man named Jeremiah Skatch, further complicates matters. However, the not-so-helpless Harry eventually triumphs over the real villain and apologizes to those he has wrongly blamed. Avi began writing *The History of Helpless Harry* as a tragedy about a boy whose fearfulness makes him evil. Somewhere along the way, his sympathy for Harry took over. As it turns out, those who are truly responsible for Harry's misdeeds are his parents and all of the other adults who refuse to regard him as the capable, resourceful person he really is. Like so many of Avi's books, this one revolves around the failure of adults to treat children with respect.

Conflicts between parents and children turn up in Avi's serious fiction also. *Wolf Rider*, based on Avi's true-life experience of receiving a crank phone call, tells the story of Andy Zadinski and his efforts to find the anonymous phone caller who claimed to have killed a woman. The police tell Andy to leave matters to them, but Andy doesn't think that they are taking the situation seriously enough. As Andy becomes more and more preoccupied with the anonymous caller, his father, the police, and his school guidance counselor begin to believe that Andy is the disturbed one. *Wolf Rider* is a psychological thriller, but it is also the story of a young person who can't agree with or trust the adults he should be able to depend on for help. Andy and his father seem close, but their relationship becomes strained when the widowed Dr. Zadinski begins to date a woman just at the time when Andy needs him most. In the end, Andy faces the anonymous caller alone, and the results are chilling.

Sometimes I Think I Hear My Name explores strained parent-child relationships in a less suspenseful but equally poignant way. When Conrad's actor parents divorced years ago, they sent him to live with his doting aunt and uncle in St. Louis. Since then, he has always spent vacations with his parents in New York. Now, however, his aunt and uncle are insisting on sending him to England for spring vacation. All Conrad wants to do is see his parents. In a daring move, Conrad slips away from the airport when his plane is on a layover in New York. Unable to reach either of his parents by phone, he drops in on Nancy, whom he met at a travel agency in St. Louis and who is now home on vacation from the private school she attends in St. Louis. As Conrad and Nancy track down first his father and then his mother, he comes to realize that his parents are not capable of thinking about anyone but themselves. It is a hard truth to face, but it does help Conrad to view his aunt and uncle as the parents he deserves to have.

While many of Avi's characters have strained relationships with parents, others are without parents at all. Children who survive in a harsh world without the protection and love of parents is another theme found in many of Avi's books. His historical novels, in particular, are full of orphans, characters who must make their own way in the world.

Encounter at Easton is the tale of indentured servants who have been forced to leave their families and to work in America because of a petty crime. In *Captain Grey*, the hero's mother is dead and his father has gone mad. The central character of *The Barn* is brought home from boarding school because his widowed father has had a stroke that has left him unable to talk, walk, or care for himself.

One of the most intriguing adventures experienced by one of Avi's parentless characters occurs in *The Man Who Was Poe*. In 1848, Edmund and his twin sister arrive in Providence, Rhode Island, from England with their aunt, who is trying to locate their missing mother. Soon Edmund's sister and aunt also disappear. Penniless and distraught, Edmund appeals for help to the first adult he meets. It happens to be author Edgar Allan Poe, newly arrived in Providence himself. Reluctantly, Poe agrees to help Edmund. Will he really help, or is he just looking for material for a new story? Whatever his intentions, Poe does solve the mystery. Then, retreating into the liquor that rules his life, he leaves Edmund to confront the forces of evil and to set things right. In *The Man Who Was Poe*, Edmund must not only take care of himself but also watch over the only adult who will help him. Again, Avi makes the point that children must sometimes act as the guides of adults.

Avi's most forlorn orphan turns up in *Punch with Judy*, set in the 1870s, when traveling medicine shows went from town to town entertaining folks and selling patent medicines. One day, Joe McSneed, the proprietor of one such medicine show, encounters a bedraggled orphan with no name, no family, no food, and no place to live. McSneed offers the boy a job as a company servant, and a name—Punch. To the bafflement of the rest of the troupe, McSneed calls Punch his "insurance policy." Four years later, McSneed dies and the company falls on hard times. How Punch saves the show and does indeed prove himself to be McSneed's insurance policy makes for a heartwarming story. In Punch, Avi created a most unusual hero—not very bright, not very funny, not very appealing to the people around him. None of this is his fault, of course. His life has been too hard for him to have developed any redeeming qualities except gratitude. Nevertheless, the power of one person's faith in him is enough to redeem Punch and give him the home and the family that he craves.

Whether Avi's characters are in conflict with their parents or are orphans, whether they appear in historical novels or contemporary stories, almost all of them are isolated in some way. The reasons for the isolation vary. In *Man from the Sky*, the main character has a reading disability that sets him apart. In *A Place Called Ugly*, the main character thinks differently from everyone around him. In *Bright Shadow*, the main character has magical powers that make her different.

Magic, the fight against injustice, family conflicts, parentless children, and isolation are some of the major themes found in Avi's books. Many of these themes are incorporated in his two Newbery Honor Books.

Chapter 13
Newbery Honor Books

In more than a quarter of a century of writing for young people, Avi has received many awards for his books. He has been honored by the British Book Council, the Mystery Writers of America, and the International Reading Association, among others.

Perhaps the greatest honor was the selection of two of his books, within a two-year period, as Newbery Honor Books. Every year, American librarians select one book to receive the Newbery Medal for excellence in children's literature. They choose a few other books to be Newbery Honor Books. Avi's Newbery Honor Books are *The True*

Confessions of Charlotte Doyle (1990) and *Nothing but the Truth* (1991).

The two books couldn't be more different in subject matter, characters, setting, and style. Yet both treat many of the themes that Avi has developed over the years.

The True Confessions of Charlotte Doyle is the third book inspired by Avi's move to Providence, Rhode Island. Although most of the action takes place on the high seas, the ship is bound for Providence, and Charlotte Doyle is a child of Providence.

When the book opens, thirteen-year-old Charlotte has spent the last seven years in England with her family. Now her father has been called home. He decides that Charlotte should finish the school term in England and then follow the rest of the family to Providence. She will travel with two well-respected families who have promised to serve as her guardians.

These precise and logical plans disintegrate, however, when Charlotte boards the ship in Liverpool and discovers that both families have had to cancel their travel plans. Thus, she finds herself the sole passenger on a ship run by a cruel and demented captain and served by a mutinous crew.

At first, Charlotte allies herself with Captain Jaggery because the two of them belong to the same social class and because the captain reminds her of her father. As the voyage progresses and the captain reveals his true nature, Charlotte's loyalties change. By the time the ship docks in Providence, she is barely recognizable as the pliant, timid, well-bred girl who left Liverpool.

She has undergone a profound change that will alter her life forever.

The True Confessions of Charlotte Doyle develops many of the themes that Avi has returned to over and over again. Although Charlotte's parents are alive, she is essentially an orphan. Deprived of parental protection and guidance, she alone is responsible for her own survival. This obligation to take care of herself comes with a corresponding right to make decisions for herself.

The decisions that Charlotte makes bring her into conflict with the one authority figure on the ship. Captain Jaggery is absolute ruler of the ship, the crew, and his one passenger. He wields this power with great cruelty and with little concern for what is best for himself or his ship. Charlotte is terrified of him. Yet, ultimately, she stands up for what she believes in, despite the consequences.

When Charlotte does make her stand against authority, she becomes as isolated as a human being can be. Trapped at sea with a captain whom she has defied, her natural allies should be the sailors who also despise and fear the captain. Yet Charlotte has alienated them with her early allegiance to the captain. They don't trust her or like her. To win their grudging respect and help, she must face a trial that no young woman of her time would think it possible to survive. Through this trial, Charlotte succeeds at breaking through the isolation that could have killed her.

When the ship finally reaches Providence, it would seem that Charlotte's trials are over. She is returned to her family, and her days of terror are over. Yet this is precisely when a new conflict arises, for her father refuses to believe her story of the voyage. So, like other Avi characters, Charlotte finds herself in a bitter struggle with her parents and once again isolated. Her resolution of that conflict brings about an "improbable but deeply satisfying conclusion," as one reviewer put it.

From conflict with authority to isolation, it would seem that all of Avi's major themes turn up in *The True Confessions of Charlotte Doyle*, except for magic. Yet, if you think of magic as wondrous changes, then there is magic in the novel. Although Charlotte's transformation may not be supernatural in origin, it is still a miracle.

Though adult reviewers have praised the book, Avi's favorite comments have come from young readers. Shortly after the book was published, he overheard a group of young people and their parents discussing it. "What do you think about Charlotte?" the moderator asked a young boy. "Well," he replied, "she's going to have a hard time getting married." "Exactly," thought Avi. This reader got it. Charlotte was a heroine who was not going to live a conventional life. Another reader sent a letter to Avi exclaiming, "Charlotte lives in my heart. Forever!" Responses like these let Avi know that this book touched readers in the way he wanted it to.

Avi's second Newbery Honor Book, *Nothing but the Truth*, explores the question of just what—and who—is right when a student and a teacher come into conflict.

Ninth-grader Philip Malloy doesn't care much for English—the books are boring and so is the teacher, Miss

Narwin. Then Philip has the misfortune of being transferred to Miss Narwin's homeroom. When it's time to stand "at respectful, silent attention" for the national anthem, Philip hums along. Miss Narwin sends him to the office for breaking the rule. A second infraction results in Philip's suspension from school. Philip can't see what he has done wrong. Neither can his parents. For them, it's a matter of his right to express his patriotism.

Before long, the whole town is involved in the controversy. As events spin out of control, even the national news media begin to cover the story. All Philip wants to do is get back to school so he can try out for the track team, but his refusal to apologize to Miss Narwin gets him deeper and deeper into a situation that he can't control.

Avi calls *Nothing but the Truth* a "documentary novel." All of the events are portrayed through diary entries, letters, memos, and conversations. There is no narrator telling readers what to think. Readers must decide for themselves who is right, or even if there is a right or wrong answer.

Nothing but the Truth takes place more than 150 years after *The True Confessions of Charlotte Doyle*. Its main character is a boy rather than a girl. It has no narrator, while Charlotte Doyle tells her own story. Yet despite the differences, both books develop some of the same themes.

Like Charlotte, Philip Malloy comes into conflict with authority, but Philip's conflict is not a life-or-death struggle that springs from his sense of what is just and fair. Philip's struggle begins in a thoughtless violation of a rule and escalates because he is both stubborn and uncommunicative. The adults around him are not evil, but they are just as rigid in their response to Philip as he is to various situations. Once these opponents are locked in battle, it's clear there won't be any winner.

Like Charlotte, Philip quickly becomes isolated in his struggle. Unlike Charlotte, his isolation increases as the book progresses. The more publicity his cause gets and the more people who take his side, the more he loses control of the situation and of what he really wants.

While Philip starts out with the support of his parents, it's clear from the beginning that they are too caught up in their own concerns to really pay attention to his needs. So, like many of Avi's characters, he is on his own when it comes to figuring out his life. Eventually, his refusal to do what his parents think he should do causes conflicts with them, too.

Nothing but the Truth doesn't appeal to all readers. It doesn't give any clear-cut answers and it doesn't end happily. It does make readers think, and this is one of Avi's goals as a writer.

Avi says it was exciting to have two of his books named as Newbery Honor Books. He also believes it changed his life by establishing him as a known writer. The recognition those two books received created an interest in his earlier books, many of which had gone out of print. Publishers were now interested in bringing out new paperback editions of them. Today only his first two picture books are no longer in print.

Having two Newbery Honor Books also changed how Avi viewed himself as a writer. The fact that he was considered somebody worthy of attention and that he was now being read by large numbers of people put pressure on him in a good way—pressure to keep writing and to stay true to his goals for his writing.

Chapter 14
Avi Today

These days, Avi lives in a large, old house in Providence, Rhode Island, with his wife and two cats, a black male named Felix and a gray-and-orange female named Charlotte.

The Providence Preservation Society uses Avi's books as part of its guided tours for students to help young people appreciate the history of the city. In the spring and the fall, tour buses regularly pull into the narrow street in front of Avi's historic house and drop off hundreds of students for a firsthand look at the setting of *Something Upstairs*. Sometimes, if Avi sees a group tour outside his house, he goes out and chats with the students about writing.

Avi's family now stretches from the east coast to the west coast of the United States. His brother Henry lives not far from Providence in a suburb of Boston. He is a doctor and professor at Tufts University School of Medicine, where he does research in the field of immunology. Henry has two grown daughters, both of whom work in adult education. Henry and Avi see each other at least once a month. They spend their time together talking, sometimes taking long walks as they talk. For many years, Henry viewed Avi as "the younger brother." Now he sees his brother as an equal.

His sister Emily, a poet, reviewer, and biographer, resides in San Francisco. She also has two grown children—a daughter who teaches art at an elementary school and a son who is a film student.

Although Avi and Emily live on opposite sides of the country, emotionally they are much closer as adults than they were as children. Although they see each other infrequently, they talk on the phone a lot, and there is always a good deal of laughter in their conversations. Recently, Avi and Coppélia spent a summer in San Francisco and saw a lot of Emily. Together they went on picnics, took train rides, attended movies, ate at restaurants, visited the farmers' market, and cooked meals for each other.

Avi's sons also inhabit two different coasts, but both remain very close to their father. Shaun, a rock musician, lives in Boston. Kevin, who used to be a performer, now manages rock bands in San Francisco. In May of 1995, the family gathered in San Francisco to celebrate Kevin's marriage. Avi's stepson, Gabriel, is a journalist in Washington, D.C.

Occasionally, Avi sees his extended family, especially at Passover and Christmas, when the clan still gathers. In 1994, Avi attended the Passover dinner at a cousin's house. Several members of the older generation had recently died, and Avi was touched that his generation was continuing the family tradition. At Christmas time that same year, the family gathered at Avi's father's house on Hicks Street in Brooklyn. It was the last holiday at the old family homestead, as Avi's father died early the next year.

What is a typical day for Avi, now that he is a full-time writer? By 8:00 or 8:30 in the morning, he is at his desk writing. At 1:00 in the afternoon, he takes a break for a jog around the neighborhood and has lunch, often with Coppélia. In the afternoon, he writes again, sometimes well into the evening. On some days he works for ten or twelve hours. Even when Avi is not at home, he writes daily on a laptop computer that he takes with him.

When he isn't working, Avi enjoys baking bread, jogging, and playing an occasional game of squash, a fast-paced racquet game played in a four-walled court. "I'm athletic now," he happily declares, recalling his childhood discomfort with sports.

Avi's main hobby is photography, though he is quick to claim that he's no expert. He likes taking nature shots, but doesn't do too well with people. "If it stays still, I can shoot it," he laughs. Part of the fun of photography for Avi is printing his own photographs in his basement darkroom.

One hobby Avi no longer pursues is collecting children's books. When he and Coppélia moved to Providence, there wasn't any room to display the three thousand volumes he had accumulated. The books sat in the basement packed away in cartons. Avi realized that the books would soon rot. As much as he loved the collection, Avi realized he didn't need it now that he was no longer teaching children's literature. Instead of selling the books, some of which had greatly increased in value since he bought them, Avi generously donated the entire collection to the University of Connecticut at Storrs. The school gave the books a thorough cleaning and placed them on the library shelves for all to enjoy.

As you would expect, Avi still spends a lot of his spare time reading, especially fiction and history. He favors English novels of the nineteenth century and American novels of the twentieth century. In fact, Avi names an author from each of these periods as the two greatest influences on his writing: the prolific nineteenth-century English author Charles Dickens and the twentieth-century American master of style, Ernest Hemingway. Dickens, who wrote long, sprawling novels filled with some of the most eccentric characters in literature, was a favorite of Avi's mother. She offered Dickens' works to her children as an example of the best in writing. Avi admires Dickens for his intricate plots and the energy of his writing. He reads Hemingway because he loves the writer's style—his use of dialogue and the precision of his sentences.

Avi doesn't read a lot of books for young people, but he does read those written by his friends. Authors for young people are frequently asked to speak at conventions of teachers and librarians. In his travels, Avi has met many other authors of books for young people. Several of them are good friends, including Jerry Spinelli, Betty Miles, Janet Lyle, Tam Conrad, and Natalie Babbitt, who lives in his neighborhood. Every few weeks, Avi and Natalie Babbitt get together for lunch and conversation.

Although Avi has journeyed to Italy, England, and Ireland, most of his traveling takes place in the United States. Every year, he visits many schools and libraries to talk to young people about writing. In fact, Avi estimates that he's made more than one thousand school visits since 1970, when his first book was published. Most of the visits have been fun and rewarding for Avi, although he does recall a few bad ones. In one situation, he walked out of the class and refused to continue his presentation. "All the kids wanted to talk about was money," he says.

What happens when Avi makes a school visit? He may discuss his writing process in depth, he may conduct a writing workshop for students, or he may read from a book he is working on.

Whatever he does in the classroom, Avi doesn't expect listeners to sit still with their hands folded on their desks. To Avi, a student who needs to yawn or cough or fidget and doesn't is more distracting than students who do what they need to do in order to be able to concentrate on his presentation. So he tells students right away that he wants them to be relaxed, that if they need to get up and sharpen a pencil, to do it. If they want to pass notes, that's all right too. Just don't talk. That is all Avi asks.

Because of his own history of frustration and distress about his writing difficulties, when Avi visits a school, he asks to speak to students who have learning disabilities. As he describes it, these students often enter the room slowly, eyes lowered, expecting yet another pep talk about trying harder. Instead, Avi doesn't say anything. He spreads out pages of one of his manuscripts covered with red-pencil marks where he has had to correct his errors. Then he points out his mistakes. "Look, there's a spelling mistake. Oh, I forgot a capital letter there. Oops, letter reversal. Look, another spelling mistake." When students realize that this well-known writer makes the same kinds of errors they do, suddenly their eyes light up and they pay attention. Avi is among friends.

Avi likes school visits because of the young people he meets. It takes a lot of organization to make a visit successful, however. Avi and Betty Miles once wrote a six-page magazine article to give teachers a step-by-step outline for planning an author visit. In the article, Avi mentioned just a few of the incidents that have caused him some anxious moments at school visits.

Once, for example, a man picked up Avi at the train station and drove him to a motel, somewhere in the suburbs of Washington, D.C. He apologized for not being able to give Avi any information about the next day's school visit. It seems the person who was supposed to pick Avi up was sick. She asked the school secretary to fill in for her. The secretary had a yoga class, so she asked her husband to do the job. "I guess you'll be picked up tomorrow morning," the man said. "Good luck!" Then he drove off.

Another time, Avi was sitting with the school librarian discussing his classroom visitations for the day. The details had all been arranged beforehand, so Avi was feeling relaxed about the day. Suddenly, the librarian said, "We hoped you would be able to say a few words to some students before we begin." Avi willingly agreed. Following the librarian through a door at the rear of the library, he found himself on a stage. In front of him were seven hundred students in grades three through six expecting him to give a talk!

Dysgraphia still has an effect on Avi's life today. Besides causing him to rewrite every manuscript numerous times, it makes him an anxious traveler. If someone tells him that he has to be ready to go somewhere by twelve noon, in the next few hours he may ask that person five times, "Is it twelve noon we're leaving?" Sometimes, while waiting for an airplane to take off, Avi will have a moment of panic and wonder, "Have I come on the right day?" Immediately, he pulls out his ticket to check. It's always the right day, but that doesn't keep him from checking his ticket several more times before the plane takes off.

Knowing that he will doubt himself for the rest of his life, Avi has made adjustments. He always keeps plane tickets in a handy pocket, for example, and he always gives in to the urge to check. Resisting the urge will only make him more anxious. Coping with dysgraphia has made Avi a compulsive checker of details. "It drives my wife crazy," he jokes.

Surely, dysgraphia has had an effect on Avi's life, but so have many other things: a family full of writers, artists, musicians, and storytellers; a home filled with books and clamorous debate about issues of social justice; a grandfather who loved American history; a tutor who told him he had interesting things to say; two children who asked for stories and listened to them avidly. All of these things have made Avi a prolific writer with boundless imagination and a never-ending supply of stories to tell. Which one will be next?

Notes

1   Avi, "All That Glitters," *Horn Book Magazine,*
    September-October 1987, p. 576.

2   *Ibid.*

Time Line

1937   Avi is born on December 23 in New York City

1938   Avi's family moves to Brooklyn

1942   Avi enters elementary school in Brooklyn

1951   Avi attends Stuyvesant High School for one quarter and transfers to Elisabeth Irwin High School

1955   Avi decides to become a writer; he graduates from high school and enters Antioch College in Ohio

1956   Avi transfers to the University of Wisconsin

1959   Avi receives his Bachelor of Arts degree

1960   Avi wins the playwriting contest at the University of Wisconsin and moves to San Francisco

1961   Avi returns to New York

1962   Avi receives his Master of Arts degree from the University of Wisconsin and takes a job as library clerk in the theater collection of the New York Public Library

1963   Avi and Joan Gainer marry

1964   Avi receives his Master of Science degree in Library Science from Columbia University

1966   Avi's first son, Shaun, is born

1968   Avi and his family spend a year in England where he is an exchange librarian; his second son, Kevin, is born

1970   Avi and his family move to New Jersey; Avi takes a job as librarian at Trenton State College; his first book is published

1976   Avi and his family move to New Hope, Pennsylvania

1982   Avi and his first wife divorce

1983   Avi marries Coppélia Kahn

1987   Avi and Coppélia move to Providence; Avi becomes a full-time writer

1991   *The True Confessions of Charlotte Doyle* is named a Newbery Honor Book

1992   *Nothing but the Truth* is named a Newbery Honor Book

Books by Avi

Things That Sometimes Happen, 1970

Snail Tale, 1972

No More Magic, 1975

Captain Grey, 1977

Emily Upham's Revenge, 1978

Night Journeys, 1979

Encounter at Easton, 1980

The History of Helpless Harry, 1980

Man from the Sky, 1980

A Place Called Ugly, 1981

Who Stole the Wizard of Oz?, 1981

Sometimes I Think I Hear My Name, 1982

Smugglers' Island, 1983
    (originally published as *Shadrach's Crossing*)

The Fighting Ground, 1984

Devil's Race, 1984

S.O.R. Losers, 1984

Bright Shadow, 1985

Wolf Rider, 1986

Romeo and Juliet—Together (and Alive!) at Last, 1987

Something Upstairs, 1988

The Man Who Was Poe, 1989

The True Confessions of Charlotte Doyle, 1990

Windcatcher, 1991

Nothing but the Truth, 1991

Blue Heron, 1992

"Who Was That Masked Man, Anyway?", 1992

Punch with Judy, 1993

City of Light, City of Dark, 1993

The Bird, the Frog, and the Light, 1994

The Barn, 1994

Tom, Babette, & Simon, 1995

Poppy, 1995

Beyond the Western Sea, 1996
    Book One: *Escape from Home*
    Book Two: *Lord Kirkle's Money*

Finding Providence, 1996

About the Author

Since graduating from Middlebury College in Vermont, Lois Markham has been an English teacher, an editor, and a writer. She has written biographies of Theodore Roosevelt, Thomas Edison, and Helen Keller. She is a frequent contributor to *Kids Discover* and has written issues of the magazine on the five senses, bubbles, Columbus, Colonial America, the rain forest, rivers, and energy. She is also the author of *Lois Lowry*, another book in The Learning Works "Meet the Author" series.

In her spare time, Lois enjoys reading, acting in amateur theatricals, tap dancing, and walking in the woods or along the beach. She loves being a mother, leading a Brownie troop, and volunteering in the library at her daughter's school.

Lois lives in Beverly, Massachusetts, with her husband and their nine-year-old daughter, Amy.